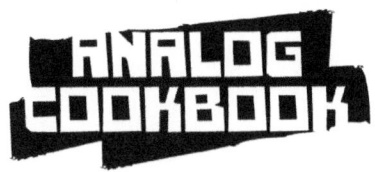

Founder/Editor-in-Chief: Kate E. Hinshaw
Editors: Andi Avery, Hogan Seidel, Gabby Sumney
Cover & Interior Design: Hogan Seidel
Analog Cookbook Logo: Sarah Lawrence's Design Emporium
Questions: hello@analogcookbook.com
Published by Analog Cookbook © 2022

LETTER FROM THE EDITORS

June 1, 2047

Dear Kate,

Just talked to Hogan, who reminded me that it's been twenty five years since Analog Futures. I suppose all these white hairs should have made the passage of time more apparent, but denial is a hell of a thing.

I started writing this because I started to consider whether or not we did a good job predicting the future. Of course, that's a less interesting question than the second question I thought of:

Did we help other artists imagine a better future that we could all build together?

I think there's always a sense that the present we inhabit was always inevitable, but nothing really is. The present is a place where dreams for the future collide with failures from the past into something new and often unexpected. The great magic trick that we artists perform is the ability to see the culmination of those things and the myriad ways they manifest—truth, beauty, knowledge, hopes, anxieties, etc.

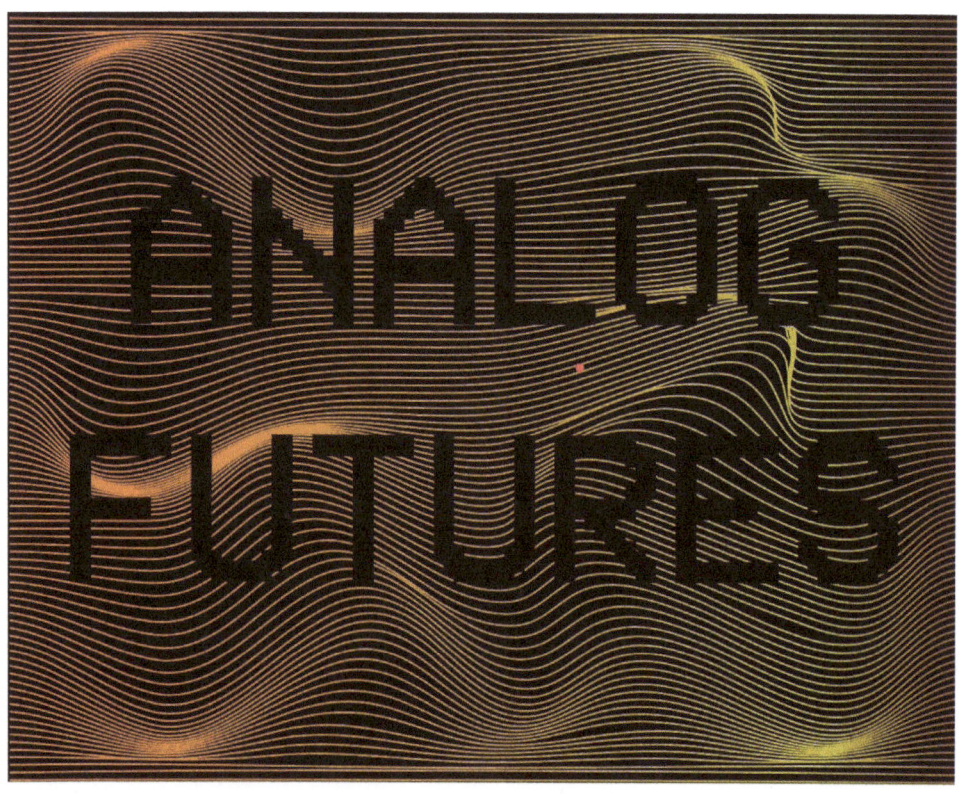

In that past that was our present when we chose to ponder the future, we were keeping analog practices alive in the face or rising prices and institutional divestment. It's not lost on me that struggle mirrors what we were being asked to do with our health and livelihoods—make individual decisions in the face of enormous community problems. In that way, Analog Cookbook was a kind of mutual aid network. We were collecting resources and getting them into the hands of people struggling to keep afloat.

I know that's an overly romantic way of looking at things, but I just can't help myself. Look at this beautiful thing you started! When's the last time you really looked at how many of us you brought together and the films your work probably helped us all make? Okay. I promise this is the end of my Kate Hinshaw stan session, but AC did bring us together; so, I'll always be so grateful of it on a human level.

One of the things that stood out to me about Futures was our refusal to be purists. Our quest to remain tactile was never so pure we would refuse digital or new media interventions. In fact, I think we were all so excited to highlight hybrid practices without any sort of litmus test or restrictions.

Want to 3D print analog parts? *So do we!*

Want to come up new ways to digitize handpainted film? *Please share that!*

Making digital memes about analog films? *Make us laugh!*

Considering the ways in which your disability complicates your relationship to your analog practice? *Sis, us too.*

Ready to weaponize your hair against predatory auteurs of the 20th century? *Tell us where to sign up.*

I wish I could have been a fly on the wall for every single person who read Futures. I wish I could have seen their reactions live. I wish I could have seen how it impacted the people who were interviewed and wrote for this gorgeous edition. I'm not saying that every issue we edited together isn't magical, but I guess you really never forget your first.

I know I said I'd stop stanning, but after twenty five years of working together and 26 since we first met, how could I not thank you? Thank you for your friendship, your endless support, your collaborative spirit, and for Analog Cookbook—the zine, the concept, the community.

Let's never stop imagining new futures together.

Gabby

ARTISTS FEATURED

10 Chantal Partamian // @Katsakh

Native to Beirut, to a Lebanese-Armenian family, I currently live and work in Quebec. Across my work, celluloid, memory, obsolescence and political imaginaries merge to reflect on erasure, denial, repetition and blur. I explore themes of justice, migration, identity, gender and conflict through the combination of a variety of practices but mainly using super 8mm. I am currently in the development phase of their next film "Odar" which also deals with fragmentation through the material condition of celluloid, and "Gaze" a super 8mm project that constructs, deconstructs, reconstructs the city and narratives, in a practice to regenerate ourselves personally and collectively. In April 2020, I started an online project of obsolete collections and temporal assemblages in an Instagram profile inspired by vinegar (@Katsakh) syndrome, the chemical degradation that occurs with cellulous acetate film.

16_João Reynaldo // Typefilm

João Reynaldo is a visual artist, writer, and researcher. With the support of Rumos Itaú Cultural 2014 subvention, João Reynaldo took part in the idealization and making of the project of digitalization of the twelve issues of Código magazine, published between 1974 and 1990 – available at www.codigorevista.org. "The Large Page," a work written between November 2017 and May 2018, and also available at the website www.erratica.com.br, inaugurates a series of typewritten works in paper sheets of 27 x 39 inches, using a 27-inch cylinder Remington Sperry Rand typewriter. Currently, João is producing a 16-mm typewritten movie: Typefilm an Armory Show.

Matt McWilliams // Building a scanner

Interview with Matt McWilliams
on open source analog resources.
Interview by Hogan Seidel.

Online content only ----->

20_Sandy McLennan // Building an R8 Optical Printer

I am a home-darkroom-based celluloid filmmaker mostly creating with, and leading workshops in, Regular 8/Double 8mm, with sound and without. I also employ portable darkrooms to make and inform using photograms and cardboard-pinhole-camera negatives.

27_Tristen Ives// lights, camera, hair!

Tristen Ives (they/them) is a filmmaker, writer, and performer who focuses on diaristic, experimental, and performative modes for political protest. They are the recipient of Public Space One's Free Studio Residency (2019-2020), and their work has been screened at ICDOCS, Montreal Underground Film Festival, Light Matter Film Festival, Craft Culture Critique Conference, Les Femmes Underground Film Festival, and FilmScene Cinema.

34_Maureen Mulhern-White // Silver Gelatin Photograms

I was born in England and spent my early years there before moving to the U.S. where I became a naturalized citizen. I received a B.A. from Sarah Lawrence College and an M.F.A. from the University of Iowa's Writers' Workshop. I am captivated by various analog photographic techniques, including toned silver gelatin photograms, lumen prints, cyanotypes, and other cameraless processes. When I am not messing around in the darkroom I am off in the boondocks with my Holga in search of highland cattle, crows and vultures. I am generally drawn to works that combine humor and playfulness with a dash of the macabre.

40_THe Halide Project // Feature by Andi Avery

The Halide Project is a volunteer-run 501(c)(3) non-profit organization dedicated to supporting the continued practice and appreciation of film and historic process photography. Based in the Kensington neighborhood in Philadelphia, The Halide Project serves the local and global photography communities through exhibitions, educational programming (both in-person and virtual), collaborations with other organizations, and - most recently - our new community darkroom, which has a gang B&W darkroom, film processing area, private color darkroom (currently with a Jobo processor), and a dim room for alternative/historic process work.

ARTIST FEATURED

@24memespersecond is an Instagram account that has been dumping memes about experimental animation since August 2020. Interview by Hogan Seidel and Gabby Sumney.

Anne-Marie Bouchard lives and works in Québec City. She directed several experimental videos/films and installations. Her work is about exploring the mysteries and wonders of the world and questioning the way we perceive and analyze it. To sense, to feel, to be immersed, and to question: her cinema is poetry.

As an artist, I am passionate about pursuing an anti-colonial filmmaking career rooted in inquisitiveness about identity and Blackness, and our diasporic history. I want to be best known for my connection-focused approach with my subjects and my sensitivity. By pulling from history and current events, I seek to help build an archive for future generations—one that has the potential to reclaim identity and celebrate the underrepresented. I have a zeal and diligence in exploring both traditional and experimental approaches to filmmaking, while rejecting all colonial ideologies brought to me through the use of media. I now use this colonial tool to recognize myself and what the medium creates. I am interested in the intersection of self reflections, and how one's scraps can be in perfect resonance in the hands of a secondary artist and one's oppressive creation can be subverted to a reclamation and proclamation of liberty. In my project I am seeking resonance with the medium and a transformation between the medium and I.

62_ Alix Galdin // Opaline

Alix Galdin is a self-taught visual artist who approaches self-portrait and documentary through film. She experimented with alternative techniques of working on film and paper, to create still and moving images.
Since 2017, Alix has participated in several group exhibitions in Quebec and France. His photos were presented at the Gesù by Maison Photo Montréal and at the Capsule Galerie (Rennes). In 2020, she made her first documentary essay on Super 8, Sainte-Croix, distributed by the GIV. In 2021-2022, she received support from Vidéographe as part of its mentoring program.

68_ Gabriel Bryant// Reactive Experiments

Hey! I'm a London-based multidisciplinary creative that enjoys making things in lots of different ways. I enjoy experimental and process-led work.

72_ Justin Rhody // No Name Cinema

Photographer, filmmaker and sound artist living in New Mexico. Operates the PHYSICAL media label and the No Name (micro-)Cinema.

76_ Andy Ray // A Prayer for Elvis

Andy Ray started out interning at Troma's Hell's Kitchen headquarters, working as a rental clerk at I Luv Video, and writing for the Onion AV Club before heading up programming at the Austin Underground Film Festival and curating media for other groups including Kinemastik in Malta. He's made music videos for dozens of punk, garage, and psych bands and festivals such as Levitation, his award-winning documentary Mondo Fuzz played the international underground festival circuit, and his own music has been featured in Rolling Stone. He currently books Di$count $inema each month at the Blue Starlite Drive-In and DJs/plays guitar for Teenage Cavegirl while in pre-production on his debut narrative feature.

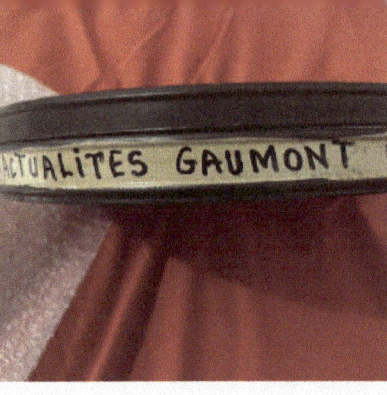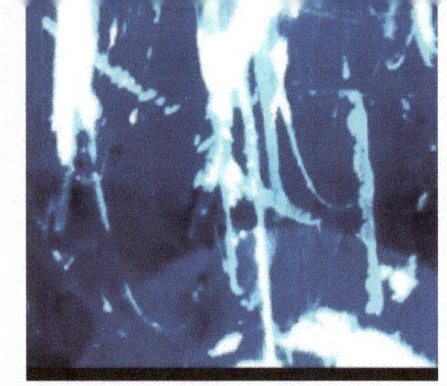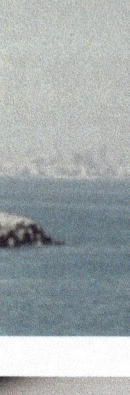
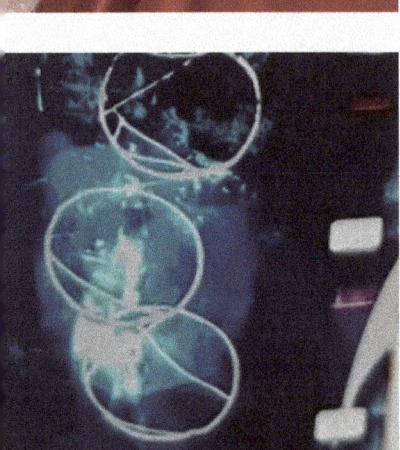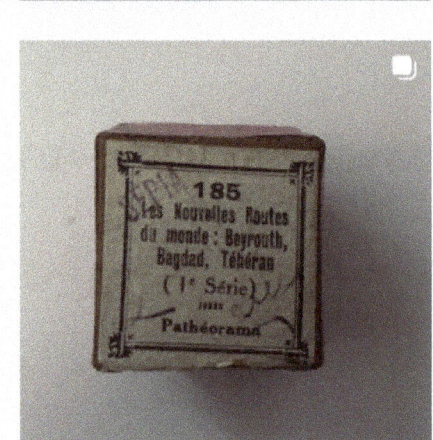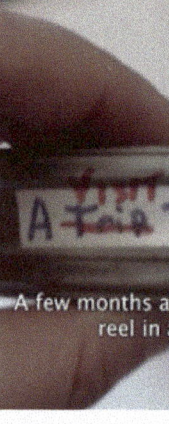
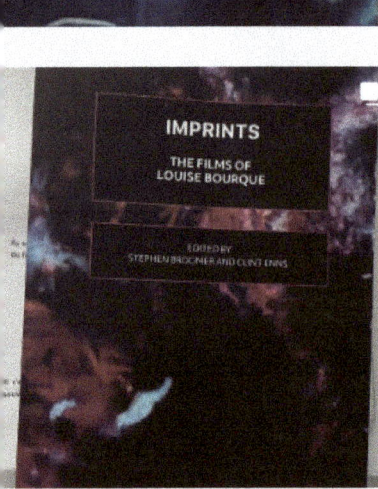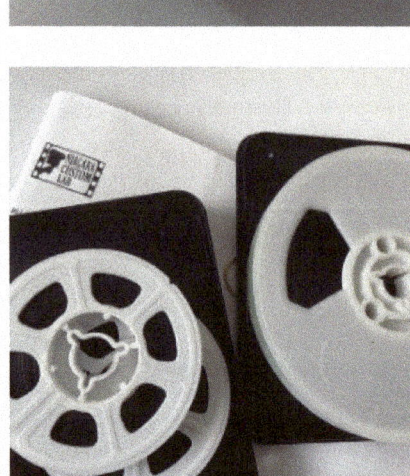
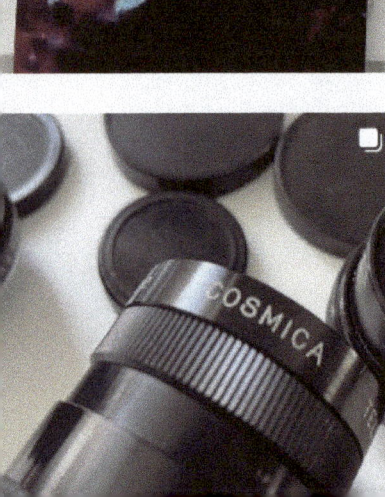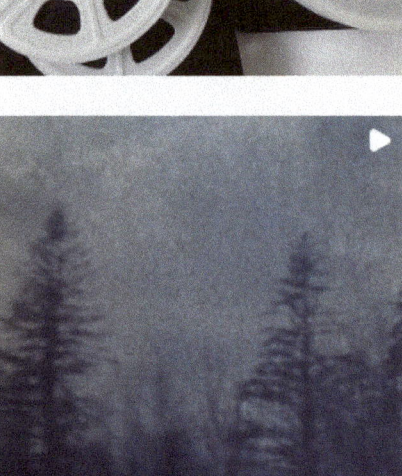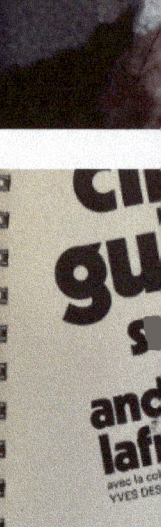

CHANTAL PARTAMIAN

@KATSAKH

"An Instagram of obsolete collections and temporal assemblages in which I showcase footage I have shot on super 8mm in Beirut, Lebanon since early 2000 but also publish many experimental capsules and DIY methods."

Tell us about your background. What first drew you to working with film?

I grew up in Lebanon in a family where everyone was and is related to film and TV production so it was quite natural for me to pick up a camera very early on and my father really encouraged it. Around the year 2000, after receiving a collection of 8mm cameras from my father, and a super 8mm projector from my mother (which had apparently belonged to her brother), I started collecting found footage and 8mm cameras from thrift spots in Beirut. Shortly after high school, I moved to France to study film, this gave me access to labs, cartridges, the possibility of shooting my own films on actual reels and so I began documenting as much of my surroundings as I could.
In summer 2006, I was back in Beirut to see my family and had my camera with me as well as cartridges in the hopes of shooting their portraits. The 2006 war broke out, I continued to shoot, I had no intention of making a film but upon my return to France after the cease fire, a friend requested that I splice my footage together and finalize it as a film in order to take part in a fundraising film projection, that is how I directed *Dear N.* My first short film entirely shot on super 8mm.

The film took a life of its own, winning a few awards, and the love for celluloid only grew from there.

What inspired the @katsakh Instagram account?

Access and sharing were mostly what inspired Katsakh. I never had full access to labs or scans or cartridges. When I was studying in France things were easier but as soon as I returned to Lebanon after my studies, that access was cut off again and so I would continue filming but would need to wait for someone heading to France or Germany in order to develop what is shot or get me more cartridges. Then most of my scans were done with a makeshift camera on projector disposition. When I immigrated to Canada 4 years ago , I brought all of my footage with me, almost 20 years of cartridges. I slowly started scanning them , duplicating them , and restoring them. I had access to labs and technicians. In addition, there were film collectors who sometimes had reels that were shot in the eastern Mediterranean on which I would bid online in an effort to have a copy, share it with those interested and ideally preserve them.

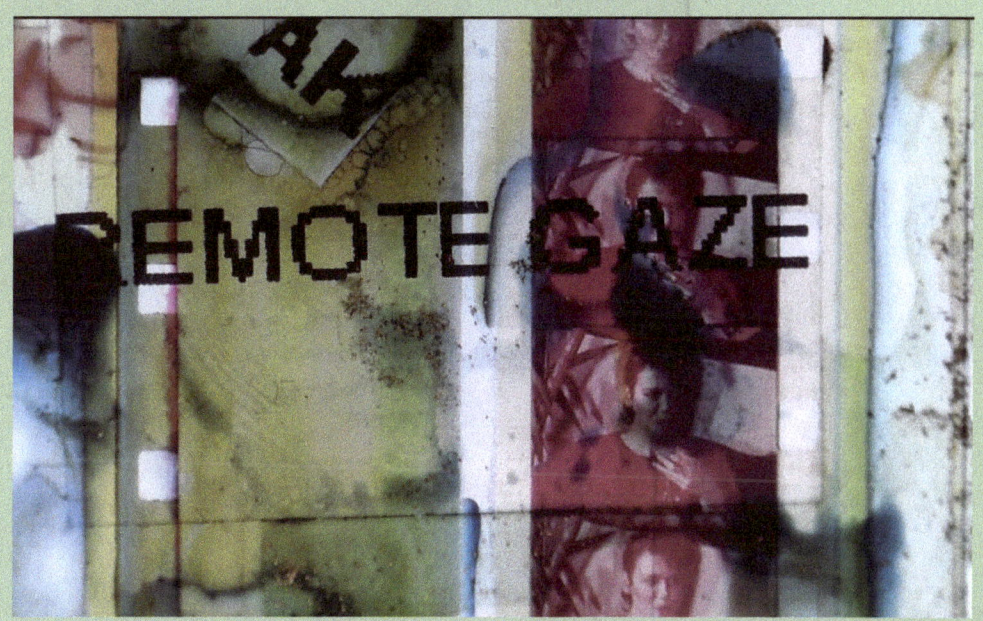

REMOTE GAZE

Working from home during the pandemic gave me the space to be around my collection and to start sorting. I decided to put it all on Instagram because it seemed like the easiest platform.

Katsakh is inspired by the obsolete, by scavenging footage, by re-editing what's found, by creating miniature films that just come to life, sometimes accidentally, sometimes not so much. It is born out of a desire to share the love of film and my collections.

Tell us about your process of scanning films damaged by vinegar syndrome.

I will sometimes use a digital microscope and I have built myself a light table and 3d printed film bases for super 8mm, 16mm and 35mm through which the reel can pass on top of the luminous plate and the frame can be picked by the microscope. It is not ideal but it helps me have an idea of what's in the cans and capture each frame. I am now trying to motorize the process of the film pull in order to make the process go a tiny bit faster. When I have found footage or acquired a print that has too much vinegar syndrome, I will not hesitate to contact a lab such as Frame Discreet to assess what can be done in order to preserve the reel and when it's an important reel I consider duplicating it but since all of these initiatives are also personal ones I have to decide which to prioritize and so on.

When working with damaged and decaying footage, it's as if you're creating a whole new world–creating new narratives within these old frames of footage.

What do you hope to achieve through this way of working?

One of the reasons I also started katsakh was because I wanted a space where I can showcase miniature creations, scratches, films that are the length of 7-10-20 seconds tops. A space for little formal experimentations.

A lot of the found footage but also parts of my archive are just as good showcased as they are and not intervened on. Other times I would get inspired and end up with a process of recycling images, transforming narratives.

There are also times where I just gather scrap or one frame leftovers and just glue them together, one after the other almost blindly and watch what feelings they evoke like some rudimentary Kuleshov effect. The formation of something despite the lacuna.

I am also constantly thinking of what it means to use other people's archives, or appropriating images, that is why for now

most of the content is that of my own while I come to terms and understanding of what it means for me to recontextualize someone's family films for example.
How to reclaim footage shot in our region as well and reinterpret or critique it from a different positionality and gaze is another concern of mine. Every reel and can has the potential to be ideologically loaded.

In addition, I might sometimes be less interested in the origin of the object rather than its trace and in other times, get obsessed by the total opposite. What draws me to it all is the idea of something that has transcended or survived, an object in its duration as much as an object from the past. The fact that my relation or feelings towards a reel can be so diverse and sometimes even conflicted is what drives my interest in the materiality of what is inscribed in the image but also beyond.

With @katsakh you're archiving materials in a digital space that could one day perish. How does this play into your work?

The entire experiment or page revolves around temporalities and the obsolete. I am well aware of the perishable nature of the platform. A lot of its content is also tangibly stored in cans however some of the experiments are definitely only finalized on digital. When I was about 6, my father's film studio was bombed during the Lebanese civil war and they lost all of their 16mm, 35mm and analog archives as well as many if not all of their equipment. This sentiment is something I carry, the possibility of absolute loss. It's definitely a source of many years of anxiety but also something I am trying to make peace with and film offers me that

> "When working with damaged and decaying footage, it's as if you're creating a whole new world–creating new narratives within these old frames of footage."

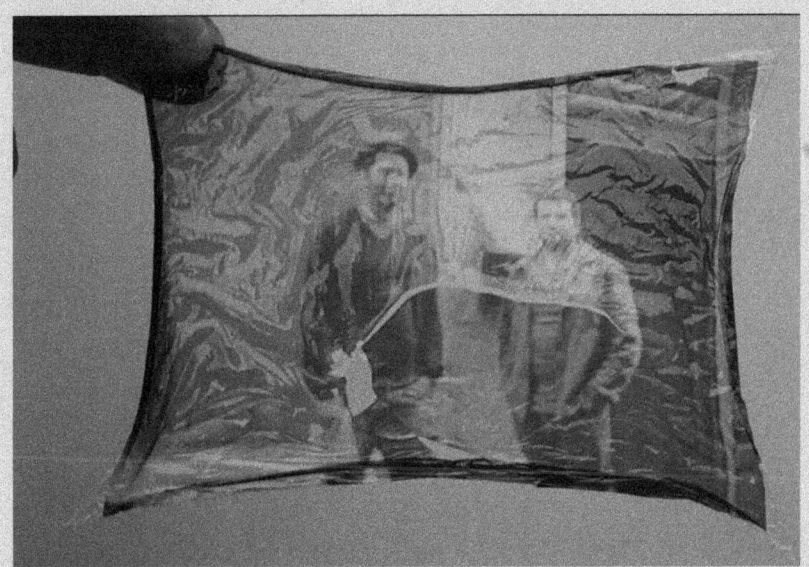

solace, it trains me to also understand the perishable and ever transformative nature of things.

There aren't many people that I know of that are thinking about preservation of film in conflict areas or countries that do not have the institutions or infrastructure (if you are out there please reach out I would love to know, hear, learn more) and I believe that is something that needs to shift, otherwise the majority of what is transmitted to future generations will reflect only that which belongs to the power structures and the privileged. Cultural producers need to have a critical perspective.

As an artist who works both within analog and digital realms, how do you view the future of exhibition? Do you plan to present more work on social media?

I do believe that social media offers an opportunity for representation especially in regions where there are no particular institutions that are interested in experimental film or even analog film or that do not have means of preservation of reels and archives and so on. Online platforms could create, albeit temporarily, a potential space for reunion, archiving, and hopefully also attract interest from festivals and institutions which in their turn, by adopting films from different geographies, showcasing them, giving them an audience, can take part in their preservation.

What's next for you?

Currently, I am working on the finalization of a super 8mm, 16mm and analog experimental short based on pornographic found footage from the 80s in contrast to the homoeroticism of the Lebanese civil war.

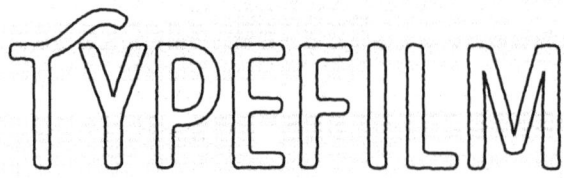
TYPEFILM

AN ARMORY SHOW

João Reynaldo

"When I hear a sentence, I hear feet marching." Thoreau

Typefilm an armory show was the title I found to name the experience of making a film typed directly onto celluloid.

As we know, the Armory Show was an international modern art exhibition inaugurated in New York in 1913. The show was held inside a building constructed with the intent of being the city's first-ever arms deposit not to use medieval fortress design as a reference. The final paragraph of the introductory text of the inaugural catalogue contains the following phrase (from Frederick James Gregg): "Art is a sign of life. There can be no life without change, as there can be no development without change. To be afraid of what is different or unfamiliar is to be afraid of life. And to be afraid of life is to be afraid of truth, and to be a champion of superstition." It strikes me how, more than a century following the staging of this exhibition

– whose organizers even produced a line of publicity lapel buttons advertising "the new spirit" – we continue to live alongside champions of superstition and consumers of hydroxychloroquine in the fight against COVID-19.

But, in any case, along with making reference to an international modern art exhibition, the title Armory Show can suggest the presentation of "ammunition" whose source is a typewriter – the set of types signaled on such a machine's keys.

The idea for making Typefilm an armory show emerged from the usage of typewriters in my artistic practice. Before I began typing through the quantity of approximately 50 meters of 16mm celluloid film stock, I would type on diverse kinds of paper of varying dimensions, as well as on a wide range of surfaces that included onion skins, cotton wads, bird feathers, pieces of tree bark, pieces of solar protective film, discartable toilet seat coverings, and carnival confetti and streamers. And it was in fact precisely the act of typing on a Carnaval streamer found in the city center of Rio de Janeiro in February of 2017 that gave me the idea of typing on celluloid film.

Typefilm an armory show is a cameraless animation work, meaning that the images are inscribed directly on the film stock without additional recording. (As a side note, I observe that this year I am creating a different version of the work that will be photographed frame-by-frame with an analogic film camera.) During initial tests, I perceived the difficulty of affixing printed characters onto the material's plastic membrane, and I also discovered different printing qualities that were pertinent to the two kinds of typewriters I was using – mechanical and electric. The print type of the mechanical machine appears in more irregular fashion than does that of the electric typewriter, which is the case for essentially two reasons: The intensity with which the type hits the surface of the film, and the qualities of the typewriter ribbon.

The intensity with which the mechanical typewriter's type hits the surface can vary depending on the strength or lightness applied in the act of typing. Such variation does not occur with the electric typewriter, whose intensity is standardized regardless of the force applied to the key. Consequently, the types printed by the mechanical typewriter can appear with more or less ink, while those printed by the electric model appear with consistent ink levels.

Regarding the ribbons, we can observe that the mechanical typewriter utilizes nylon in its ribbon composition and that the electric makes use of polyethylene. It was possible to verify during some of the Typefilm projection tests that the nylon mesh appeared to granulate the character of the writing. This observation led me to choose the electric typewriter with which I made the film, as the polyethylene ribbon helped the typed characters appear more compact during projection.

As for the fixation of the printed characters (a fastening which was made necessary due to how any physical contact with the celluloid could accidentally erase, obscure, or blot them out), I decided to use transparent Scotch tape as covering. I applied the tape onto the film stock soon after typing each frame. Another inconvenience and curiosity lay in the difference between the spacing of lines on the typewriter and the perforations of the 16mm film, which determined the irregular alignment of the text from one frame to another. I had to deal with this irregularity during the entire process of making the film. Furthermore, the film stock would constantly shift its position in an unstable way after being placed into the typewriter's cylinder, something that does not happen, for example, with a traditional letter-sized sheet of sulphite paper.

At a certain point in the process I was able to define a number of characters for each frame, which I did by taking into account the dimensions of the frame as related to character size and possible vocabulary choices: Eight characters per frame, with four characters occupying each one of two parallel lines.

I created the script at the same time as I made the film itself, and therefore used two typewriters, which allowed me to see all of the frames contained on the film reel together on one page. This visualization helped stimulate me to work on the repetitions of some sequences, to add or subtract frames, and to alter the text. In the process I was able to create standards of duration, something that would be inviable if I were to refer to sequences by depending entirely upon my memory or by manually unspooling the film from its reel and consulting them. I also considered important (above all, during the early stages of the work) the use of a metronome to imagine the durations of frames marked in the script and the ultimate legibility of the sequences – each of which, in keeping with cinematic tradition, would unfold at a rate of 24 frames per second.

A great deal of the work involved in building the text demanded research in online dictionaries in search of words with specific numbers of characters and/or that began with one letter or another. I also consulted books such as Lewis Carroll's Doublets, a Word-Puzzle (1879).

I wish to highlight how, beginning at Frame #738, I transcribe the solution that Carroll provides to the combination of NAVY with ARMY, while adding the word MARY – this doublet, alias, was originally published in the magazine Vanity Fair on May 24th of 1879. Another noteworthy citation, which appears in Frame #4048, is motivated by the immediately preceding sequence of frames containing the words "moon" and "zinc". This is a translation into idiosyncratic English of a fragment of the lyrics of the song Chão de estrelas ("Starry Floor"), which was written in collaboration between Silvio Caldas and Orestes Barbosa, originally recorded in 1937 on 78 rpm by the Odeon studios in Rio de Janeiro, sung by Silvio Caldas with accompaniment from Benedito Lacerda and his regional band, and released as the B-side of the song Arranha-céu ("Skyscraper"). The fragment goes, "but the moon pierces our zinc and splashes stars on our floor". (And, for those interested in knowing the original Portuguese-language version, it goes, "mas a lua furando o nosso zinco salpicava de estrelas nosso chão".) At this moment I feel transported to what is commonly known as the Golden Age of Brazilian music and move to modify Thoreau's words: "When I hear a sentence, I hear a song." I now wish to highlight two of the innumerable efforts that other people have made to relate typewriters and film: Friedrich A. Kittler's book Gramophone, Film, Typewriter (1999), and the "paperfilms" made by Peter Kubelka that resulted from the usage of a typewriter for creating "cinematographic phantasies". Per Kubelka (referring in particular to the creation of typewritten scores for his film Arnulf Rainer), "The typewriter prints a regular chain of symbols on paper, just like the film projector projects images in regular succession on the cinema screen."

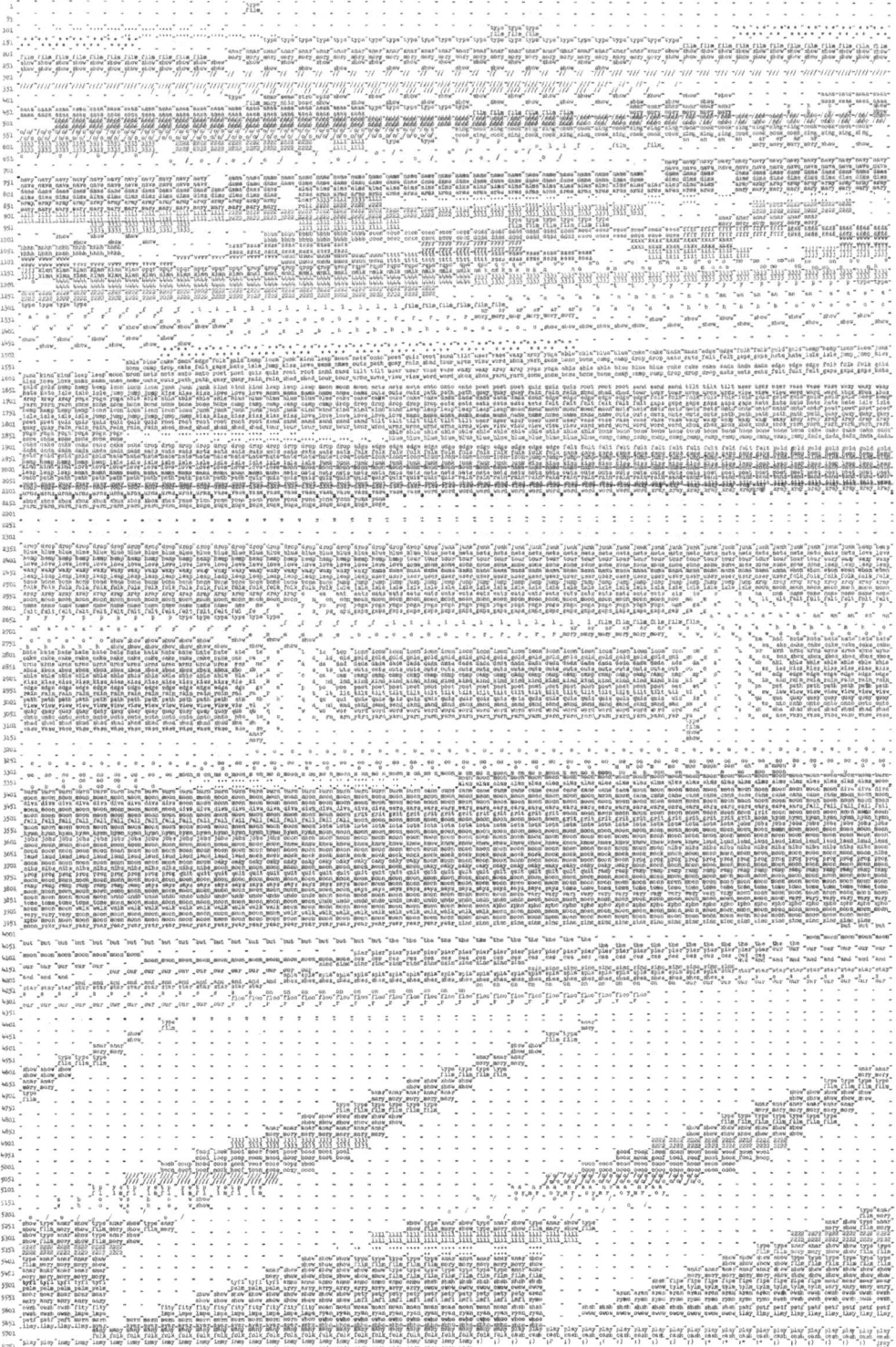

19

HOW TO BUILD AN R8 OPTICAL PRINTER

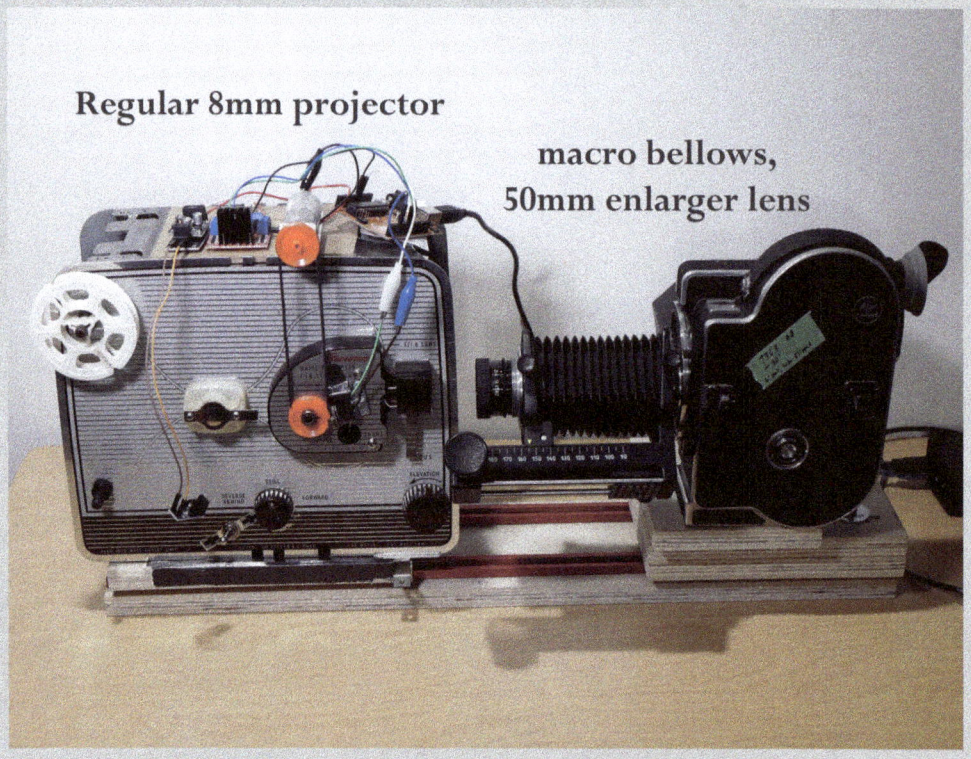

Regular 8mm projector

macro bellows,
50mm enlarger lens

BY SANDY MCLENNAN

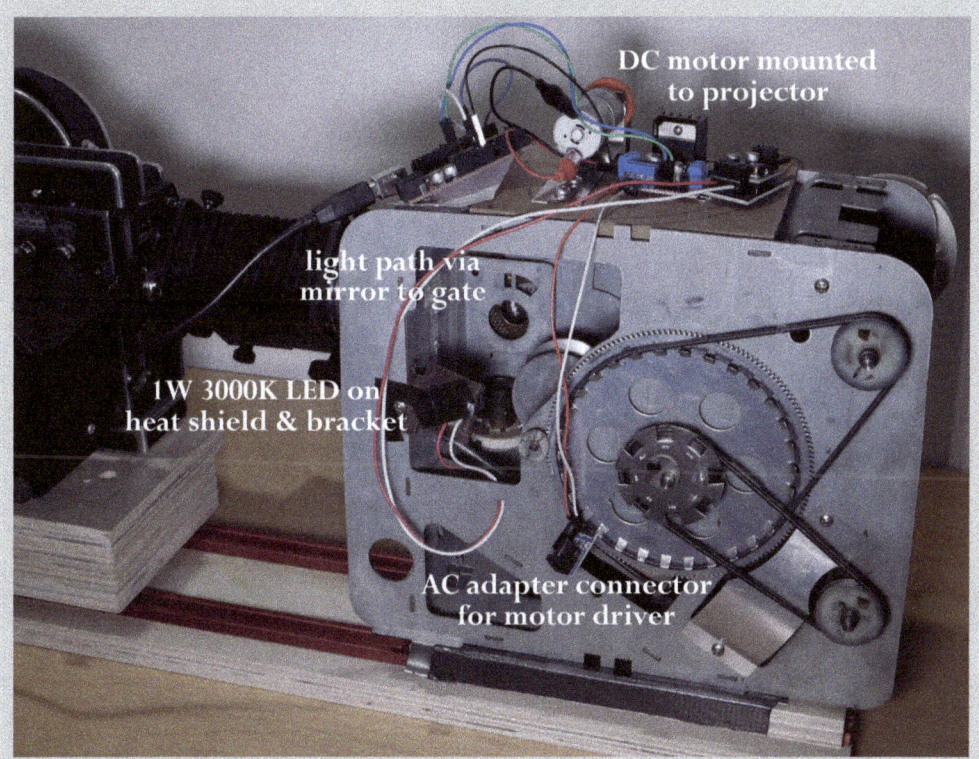

DC motor mounted
to projector

light path via
mirror to gate

1W 3000K LED on
heat shield & bracket

AC adapter connector
for motor driver

I had never heard of an optical printer with a Regular 8mm film camera. I had the idea that there ought to be one (at least) and that I could use it in my filmmaking. I thank Penny McCann for suggesting I apply for a Canada Council for the Arts grant to research and build one, and Matt McWilliams, without whom I would not have been able to get one made. I see by the email archive I wrote to Matt on March 12, 2020 (appears as quite an ominous date now), saying I got a grant and might I engage him (for a pittance) to help me out. He agreed. Over the next few months I did, with much Matt help, build a Regular 8mm optical printer.

The idea is to take advantage of the unique format that is Regular/Double 8mm (the film that goes around twice!). In particular, the Double 8 format was in mind, imagining re-photographing 16mm (or Double 8) or Regular 8mm frames to place them purposely on either side of the 4-frame Double 8 image. One could plan, or rejoice in chance, how the multi-frame movie might look and feel.

The camera is a Bolex H-8 REX-4, which I bought from Jean-Louis Seguin. I modified two different projectors to provide the "negative": a Noris 200-II 16mm (from a take-it-if-you-can-use-it box of film stuff) and a Kodak Model-1 Regular 8mm (from a Kijiji enquiry that became a gift: "oh, you would use it?!").

The camera is advanced (forward or backward) one frame at a time by a DC motor connected to the 1:1 drive shaft on the REX-4. The projector is advanced one frame at a time by a DC motor connected to a shaft of the film transport mechanism. The DC motors are

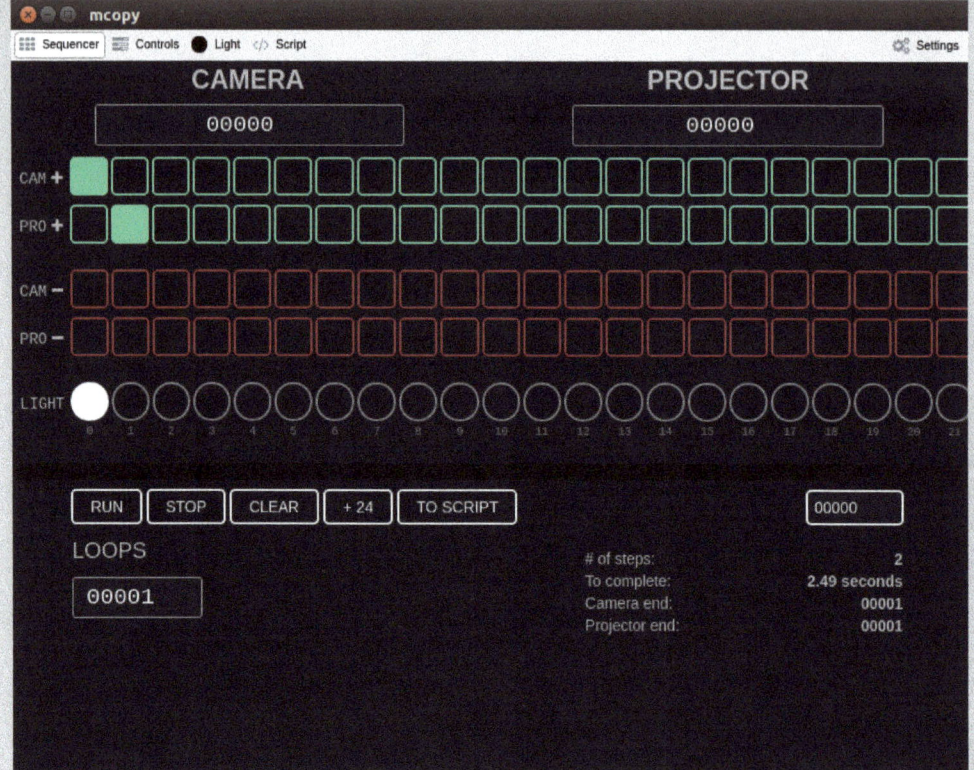

activated by an L298N motor driver and an Arduino UNO or Nano microcontroller. The automation of steps is programmed by Matt's MCopy software.

The trickiest part was creating a switch mechanism (and holding it firmly in just the right place) that would open and close relative to the projector advancing exactly one frame. Then to have the open/closed message communicated and the motor started or stopped. On the Kodak I nipped a bit out of the pulley so at that point the microswitch opens, on the Noris I dabbed a bit of hot glue on the pulley to press the microswitch closed at that point.

Other new tricks for this old dog were devising and building a base, hacking pulleys and belts so the motor would turn the projector shafts, guessing and buying wrong and eventually right electronic components, connecting all the wires, then getting my head in to the software programming way of thinking. It was not my usual brainflow and it was frustrating, so required patience and time. In the end I learned a bunch about microelectronics and how to edit the Arduino language to make the machines do what I needed and how to troubleshoot when they didn't.

To advance the Bolex transport, Matt modified the innards of an AC animation motor Jean-Louis gave me, installing an Arduino Nano, motor driver and 3D printed shaft with switch to detect one rotation.

The projector's lamp is replaced by a 1W 3000K LED and driver, which could perhaps have its intensity controlled or be replaced by an RGB LED. For now I tape neutral density and/or color correction filters (cut from a Rosco sample pack courtesy of Karl at LIFT, Liaison of Independent Filmmakers of Toronto) between the lamp and the "negative" (or whatever you have in the gate).

The camera and projector sit on their own platforms which independently slide on aluminum rails. The height of the camera lens and the projector gate had to shimmed in line with each other. I tried a macro bellows (eBay from Ukraine) adapted for C-mount on the camera, with an M42-thread 50mm enlarger lens. This may work for reducing or enlarging the negative, but for 1:1 framing I used a set of Bolex macro extension tubes from Jean-Louis and the 50mm enlarger lens. This setup has an extremely shallow focus plane and trying to nail it by wiggling a wood platform is awkward and annoying – to be modified in future with a screw/crank system.

Other improvements to the setup would be assembling the projector's electronic components in a box, similar to what Matt did with the camera animation motor box. Pandemic truth be told, after doing a clip test to verify all the functions work, I felt burned out by ... you know. So writing this is a gateway to getting back to it, imagining my image ideas coming to life and the child-like feeling of a cool tool that was built from bits and pieces.

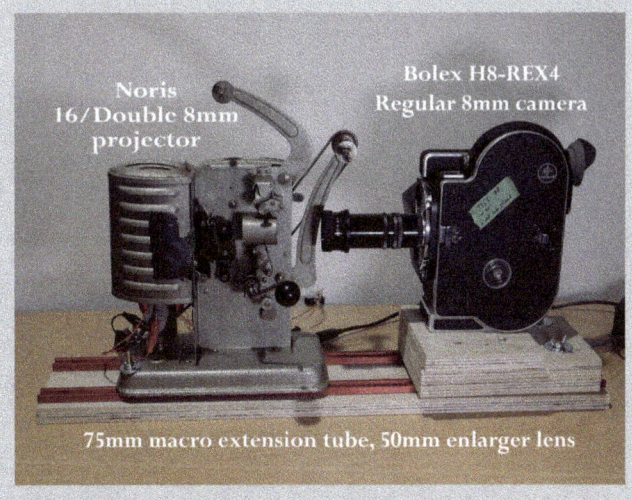

Noris 16/Double 8mm projector

Bolex H8-REX4 Regular 8mm camera

75mm macro extension tube, 50mm enlarger lens

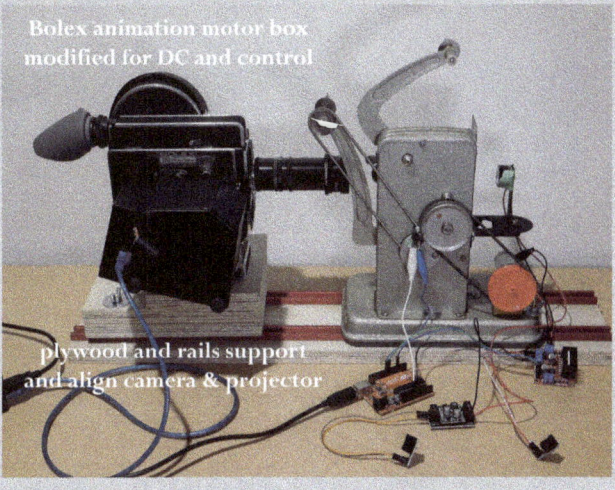

Bolex animation motor box modified for DC and control

plywood and rails support and align camera & projector

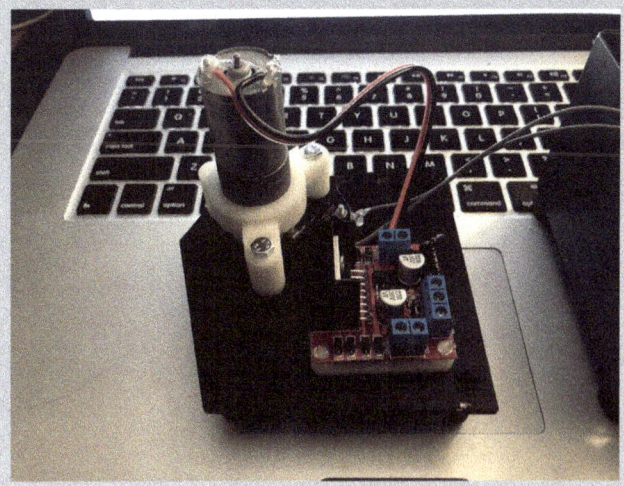

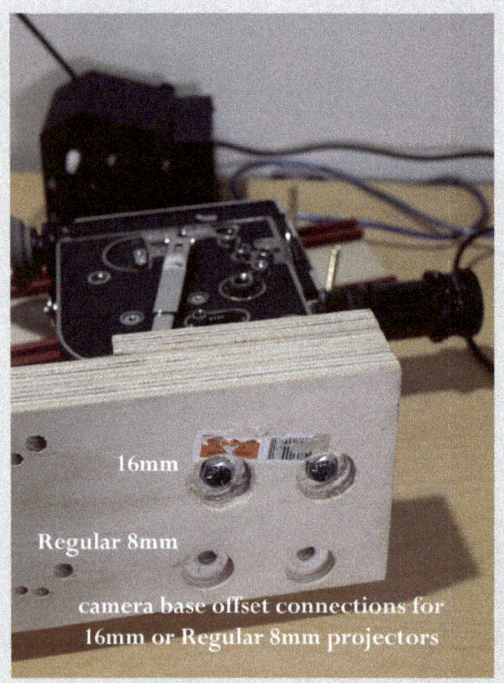

16mm

Regular 8mm

camera base offset connections for
16mm or Regular 8mm projectors

Camera Base

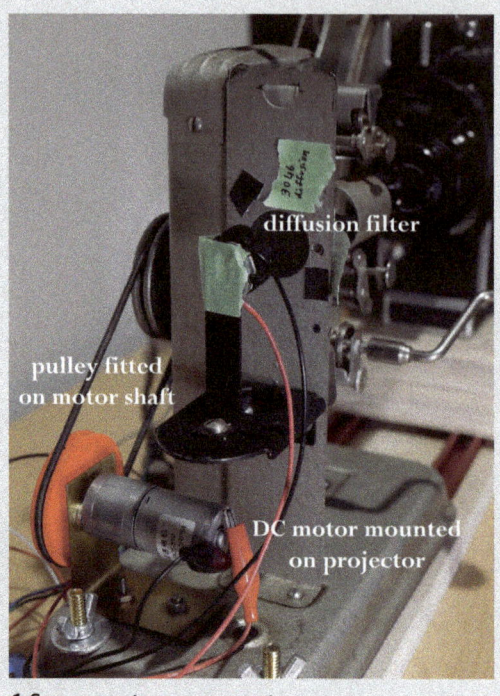

diffusion filter

pulley fitted
on motor shaft

DC motor mounted
on projector

16mm motor mount

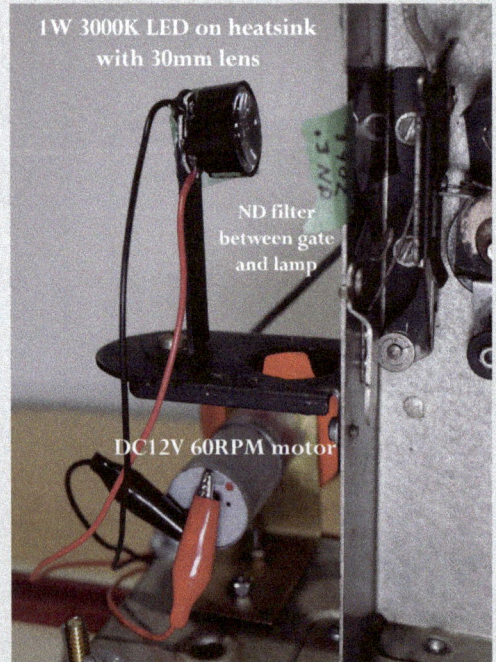

1W 3000K LED on heatsink
with 30mm lens

ND filter
between gate
and lamp

DC12V 60RPM motor

16mm lamp, motor,
and filter

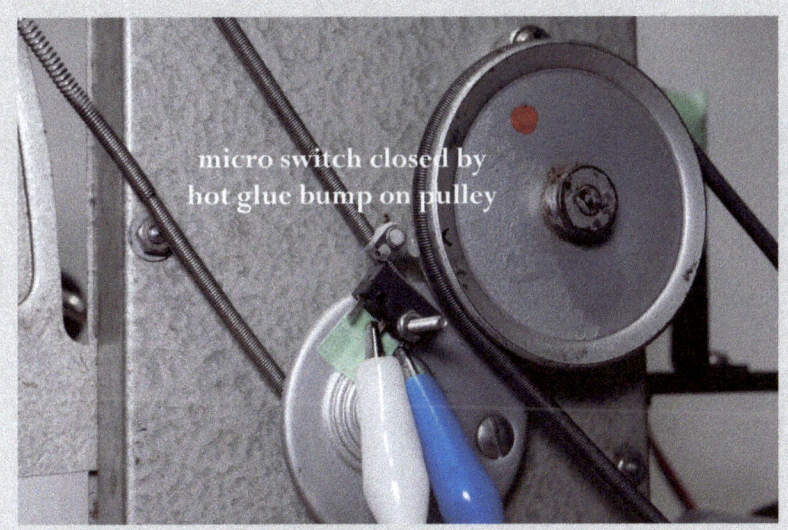

16mm microswitch

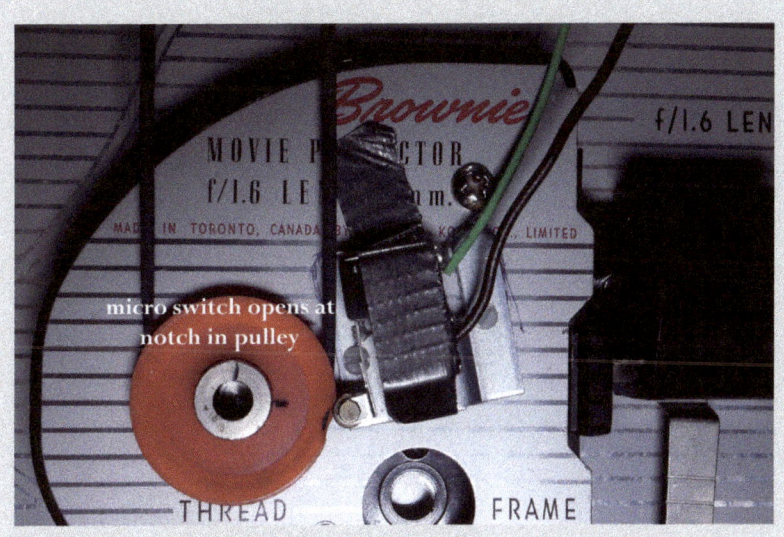

8mm microswitch

Electrical Components

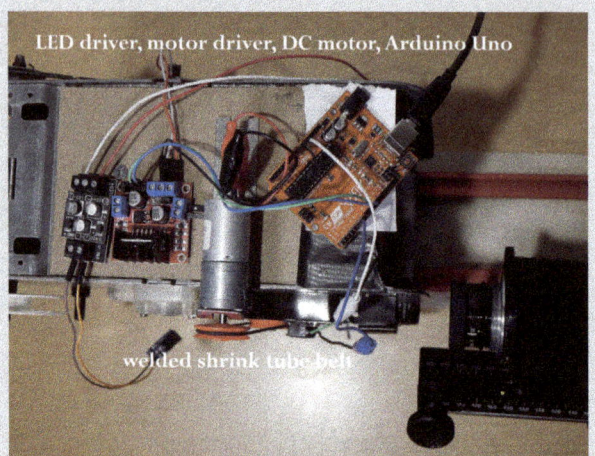

LED driver, motor driver, DC motor, Arduino Uno

welded shrink tube belt

8mm

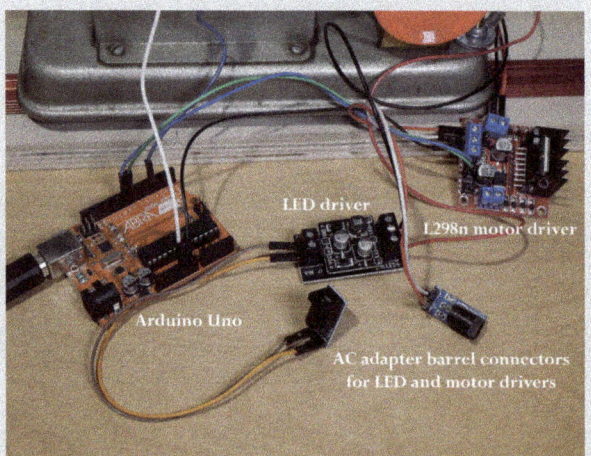

LED driver

L298n motor driver

Arduino Uno

AC adapter barrel connectors
for LED and motor drivers

16mm

Reference Links ------->

lights,

camera,

hair

Tristen Ives

lights, camera, hair! is a hybrid film which deconstructs Stanley Kubrick's treatment and abuse towards Shelley Duvall during the production of "The Shining." Using footage from the film combined with Vivian Kubrick's documentary short "The Making of The Shining," the filmmaker empathizes with Duvall's suffering on and off screen by shaving their head.

Can you take us through your process making *lights, camera, hair!?* Do you have any process photos you would like to share with us?

The desire to attach hair to film came first, but I didn't know exactly what kind of film I was going to make. I wanted my first project in 16mm to involve hair because of how gross it is. I have an intense aversion to hair, and I thought it would be beneficial to confront that disgust by working with it as it's own medium. I was also starting to question my gender identity during this time, and shaving my head was a big turning point in my journey. So attaching the hair and making something out of what once was seemed like a good way to process those actions in a meaningful way.

While I started attaching my hair onto film strips, I encountered Shelley Duvall's story and how she lost her hair due to the distress Stanley Kubrick put her under during the production of The Shining. I started to do research on these events, and encountered Vivian Kubrick's Making of The Shining, which is a short documentary showcasing behind-the-scenes footage of Kubrick's strategic plan to make Shelley Duvall go mad on set by berating her performances and guiding the crew to treat her coldly to produce a "better performance." Through an empathetic lens, Kubrick's daughter, Vivian, caught the destructive events on film. In the documentary, Shelley complains to the crew about how impossible and militant Kubrick is being, how overworked she is, and that her hair is falling out due to stress. Kubrick's actions ended up having a lasting impact on Shelley's mental and physical health for the rest of her life.

The connection of my hair and Shelley's was almost instant. I just started working and it all came together. Alongside the 16mm aspect of the film, I started to string together footage of The Shining and Making of the Shining to guide the viewer through the events. By combining both story and my hair into the film, it became a hybrid of processing and empathizing with Shelley.

What was your favorite tool you used to create this film?

My hair

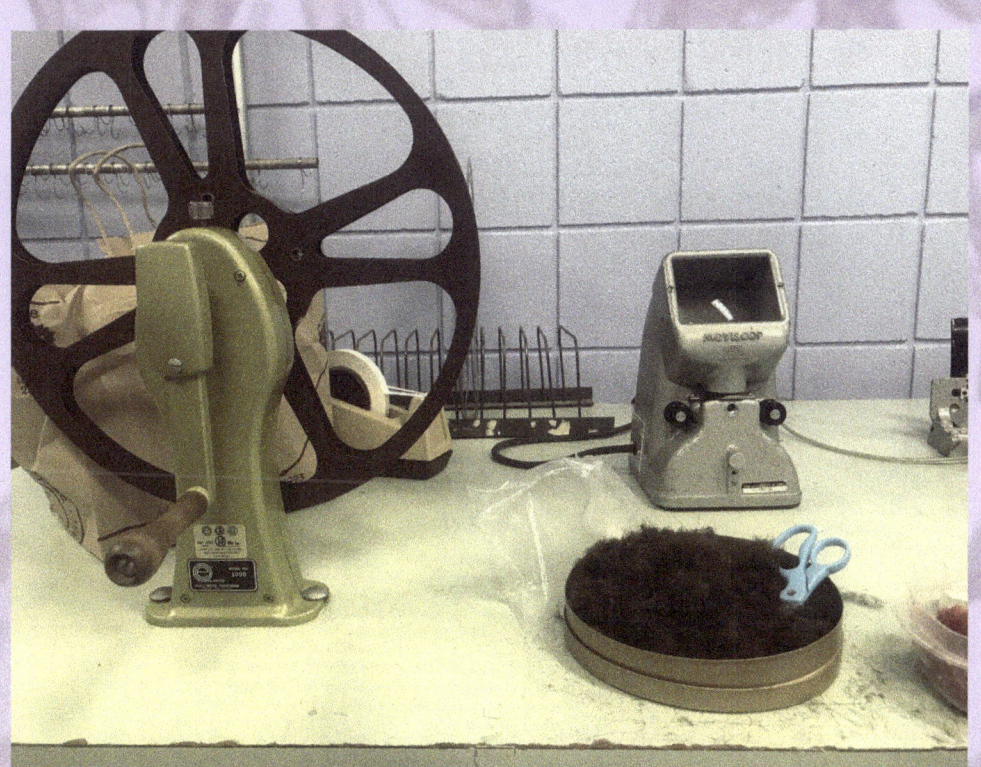

Tell us about your process making 16mm rayograms.

The decision to rayogram was for a couple reasons. I wanted to have many different tests of hair on film to see what I liked best. I ended up using each method in the film, but the biggest reason I decided to rayogram was so I didn't dirty up the film digitizer and 16mm projector I shared with my peers at the university. Understandably, they didn't want me to leave remnants that could get on their films and scratch it all up. To avoid leaving a hair trail, I spent a lot of time gluing and splicing tape onto the entirety of the film surface area to sandwich the hair in, and then eventually rayogramming since that wasn't going to affect others who were going to use

the projector. Rayogramming was definitely a learning curve for me. You know when some people say you have to learn the hard way? That was the case for me creating this film, haha. I'm a projectionist by trade and my boss would give us a couple LED lights for times when we would need a good fumble about the booth during the show. I thought this would be an okay flashlight to work with because I really didn't know about what kind of flashlights you are supposed to use. For starters, it should be a pretty dim light. So I was already off to a great start, haha. Since the flashlight was so bright, it took me four tries to rayogram correctly. I would place 10 feet of tri-x reversal film on the floor, get on my hands and knees, and rearrange each strand of hair into compositions on each frame. Once

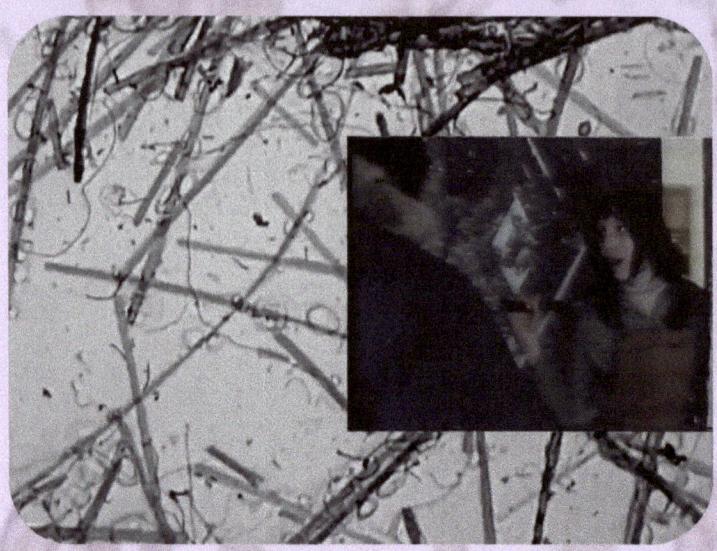

I reached the end of the film strip, I turned my flashlight on and ran from one end of the darkroom to the other end. I developed the strip and saw nothing but black. So I repeated this process four times, each time running faster across the room than before until I got the rayogram to show up.

What attracts you as an artist to investigate the bias in someone else's work? OR what do you think the role of artists is in investigating historical bias in existing work? What do you want audiences to walk away feeling or knowing about Shelly Duvall and Stanley Kubrick?

My investigation started with a need for an answer. This story ignited an intense anger in me. During my undergrad in film studies and production, it seemed that everyone was praising filmmakers such as Hitchcock and Kubrick, who are famously known for torturing their actresses by putting them in dangerous and non-consensual situations on set to produce an authentic representation of fear.

Whenever I heard these stories, I felt like my brain was on fire. I couldn't reconcile or justify how much these filmmakers were glorified. It seemed their actions were dismissed because they "made a masterpiece." Furthermore, their actions and impacts weren't even talked about, even in a classroom setting where the conversation should most definitely be happening.

A common conversation I have with viewers surrounding this film centers around the topic of separation of art and the artist and cancel culture. It was never really my intent to "cancel" Kubrick or The Shining. This film was primarily a response to and a process of my anger towards Stanley Kubrick, and more importantly, his legacy. Vivian Kubrick's *Making of The Shining* showcased mental distress you couldn't look away from or take a passive take on, and I think that has a lot to say about mental trauma that is easy to dismiss.

I did receive some coldness from my peers

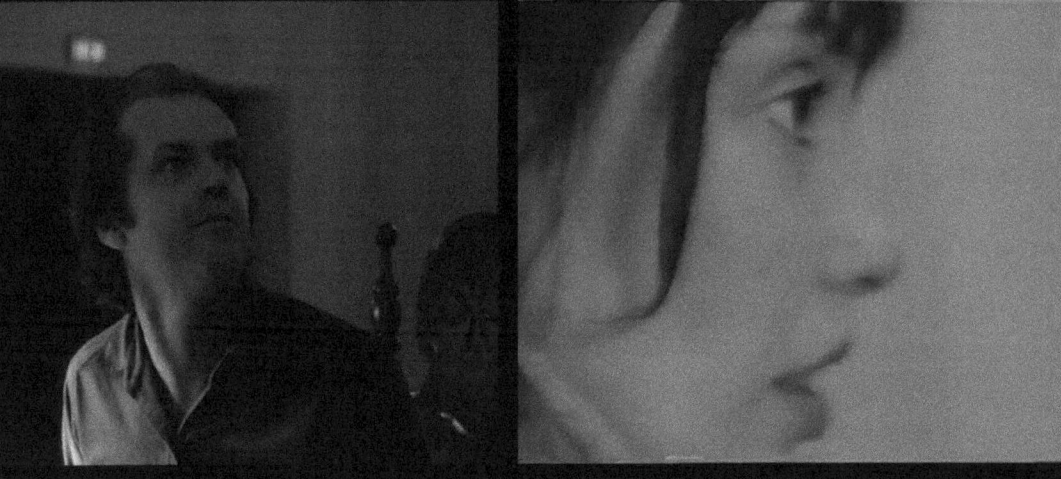

after making this film. No one likes when light is shed on the darkness of their favorite filmmakers. I've had the conversation over and over about separation of art and the artist, which is still a complex and mind boggling topic. Sometimes, there are no clear cut answers. I'm not saying you can't like the movie. It is successful in being horrifying and has a significant impact in film history. I just wanted to seek more discussion about film ethics and work that is being done right now to uncover these stories and give them the spotlight they deserve.

What do you hope for the future of analog storytelling?

In the experimental world, I think these mediums are alive and well. I definitely see a lot of my peers in this field seeking instruction and information on analog filmmaking. And there is definitely a desire to keep the art form going.

Taking a 16mm class during my undergraduate career was one of the most beneficial things I could learn and implement in my life. I built friendships that are extremely meaningful and lasting within those spaces. It gave me a much deeper dedication, appreciation, and understanding of how film works and forced me to really give time to my projects because you have to make sure you're not wasting anything due to the cost of film and processing. I hope that emerging filmmakers can create communities and spaces for all people to learn and continue this art form. I also hope that we can start to make it a more accessible medium somehow.

On a flip note to creating film, I currently work as a projectionist at SIFF and often project 35mm film. That has brought so much meaning, excitement, and pride to my life. It's beautiful and surreal to have so many people come out and see a new or archival print. And to work with many curators, programmers, and people who just collect prints or donate them to old cinemas.

What keeps you motivated/producing?

The first time I picked up a camera was to process the world around me, but to also understand myself. It's extremely telling how one decides to present information through ways of visual art. I'm always learning about myself and how I navigate the world whenever I put images I filmed in sequence. Community definitely keeps me inspired. It's so special to work with others on their films or for them to help you with yours. I feel so connected with those people and feel truly understood.

Consuming films, both old and new, also keeps me going. Especially ones that dwell in the experimental realm.

What's next for you?

My main mode of filmmaking is experimental documentary/diaristic. I always keep a camera with me, maintaining a daily practice of filming at least one thing per day. I'm constantly thinking about film - making, consuming, dissecting. It's an obsession for sure. I work with video, 8mm and 16mm. Since I'm also a projectionist, I'm kind of always somehow fiddling with film in one way or another.

I'm also pretty intermedial in art since I also love to paint, write, make sound and music, and small sculptures. Mainly, I just love creating and being in a community of people who have an intense drive to do the same. Right now, working with friends and their projects is in my immediate future.

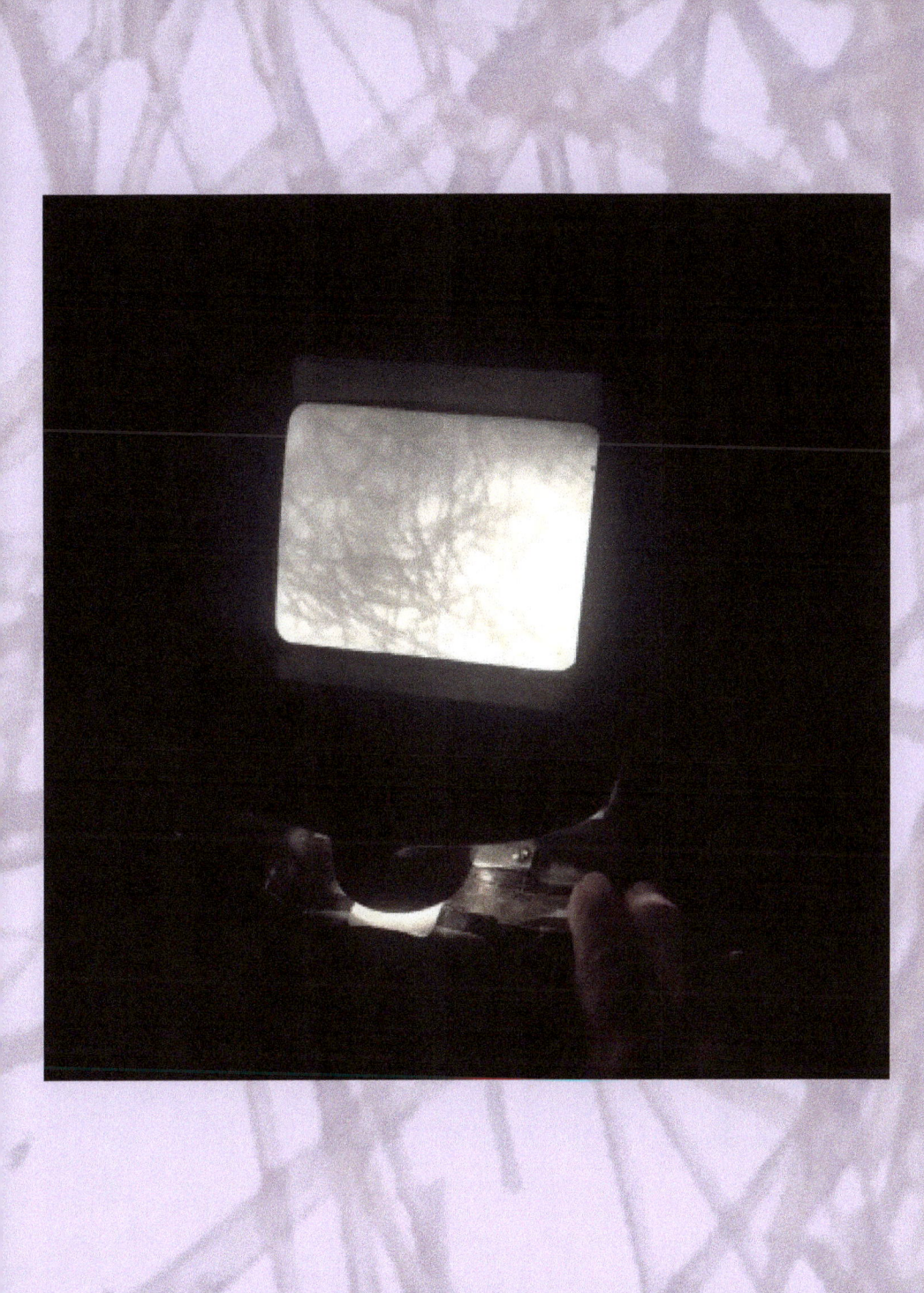

SILVER GELATIN PHOTOGRAMS

Maureen Mulhern-White

Tell us about your background. How did you first get into working with film?

My first film camera was a Nikkormat, which had been my brother's. He had a makeshift darkroom in our basement and I was intrigued by the trays, the chemicals, the final prints that emerged from this mysterious set up. This was many years ago and I stopped shooting film for a long time until I discovered the endless joys of cheap, plastic cameras. I am attracted to the unpredictability and quirkiness that defines the Holga (and other light-leaking plastic cameras).

Tell us about your process making photograms.

I worked at Harvard's Gray Herbarium Library after I had moved back to New England (I went to graduate school in Iowa) and in that magical setting I discovered the works of Anna Atkins. I didn't start making cyanotype photograms until many years later; and started with the omnipresent fern, leaf, and feather arrangement. I soon got tired of these objects and moved onto making cutouts from crude drawings that I made and I still use my cutouts in silver gelatin photograms.

What are your favorite materials to work with when creating prints?

I keep telling myself to move away from turmeric, just move on to something else, but it still has a hold on me and thus I am still using it to tone my photograms (cyanotype and silver gelatin).

Can you tell us about an accidental discovery you've made?

Because I am self-taught, everything is an accidental discovery.

What kind of art do you like to consume? Is it related to the medium you work in?

This is a great question! I keep returning to the works of Paul Klee and Franz Marc and a number of lyric poets. I don't see many dividing lines between painting, poetry, music and photography. Photograms seem to embody lyricism.

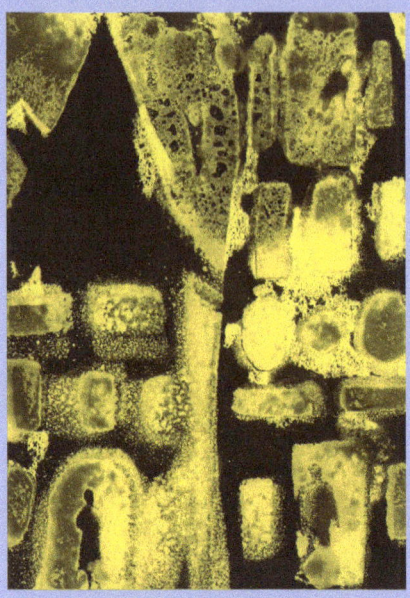

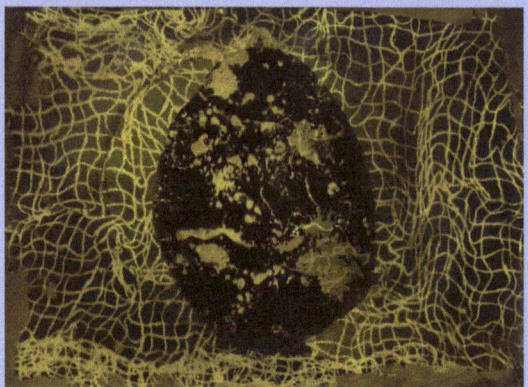

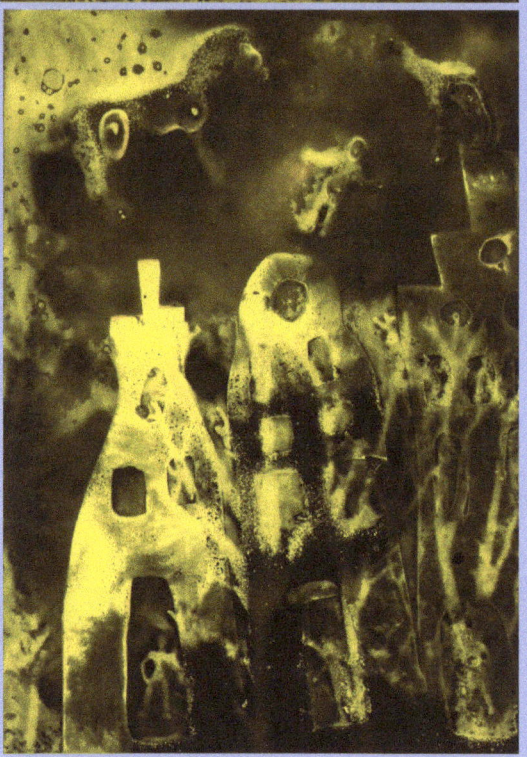

What keeps you motivated/ producing?

Experimentation is key to what keeps me going. It seems counterintuitive, but I think it's important for me to keep making mistakes because they guide my sense of what it is I am trying to achieve.

What does the future of analog technology look like to you?

I think that while digital photography and various types of editing software will continue to dominate the photography landscape, the uniquely tactile aspects of working in a darkroom will always be attractive to those who wish to have that intimate hands-on connection with their work. Playing with darkroom chemicals, adjusting light, timing of exposing, coating paper with emulsion, all of the "thingyness" of making a print will never disappear.

What's next for you?

I am trying to muster up the courage to work larger. My works are all very small. It feels daunting somehow to move out of my comfort zone but perhaps it will offer new challenges (and welcome mistakes).

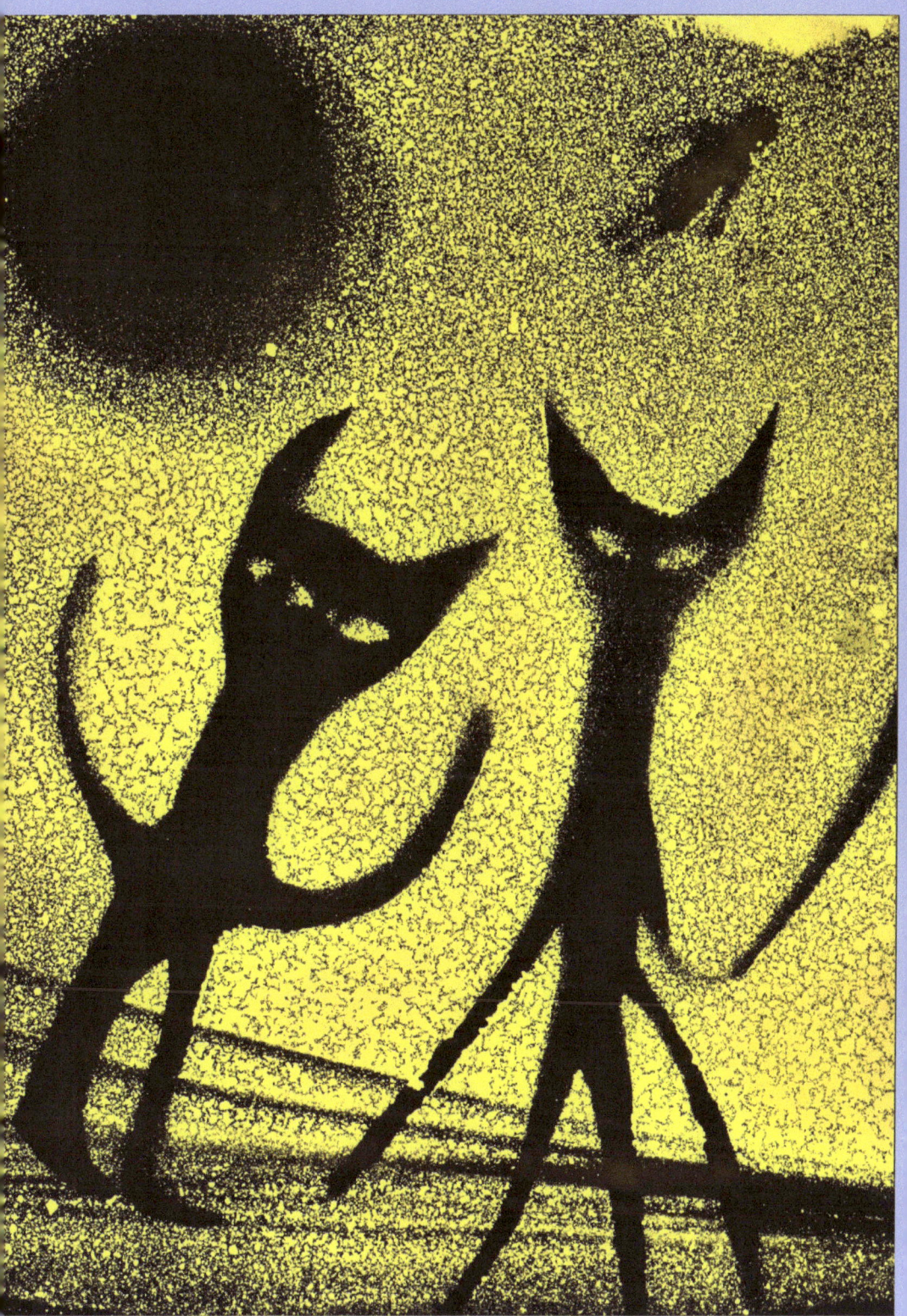

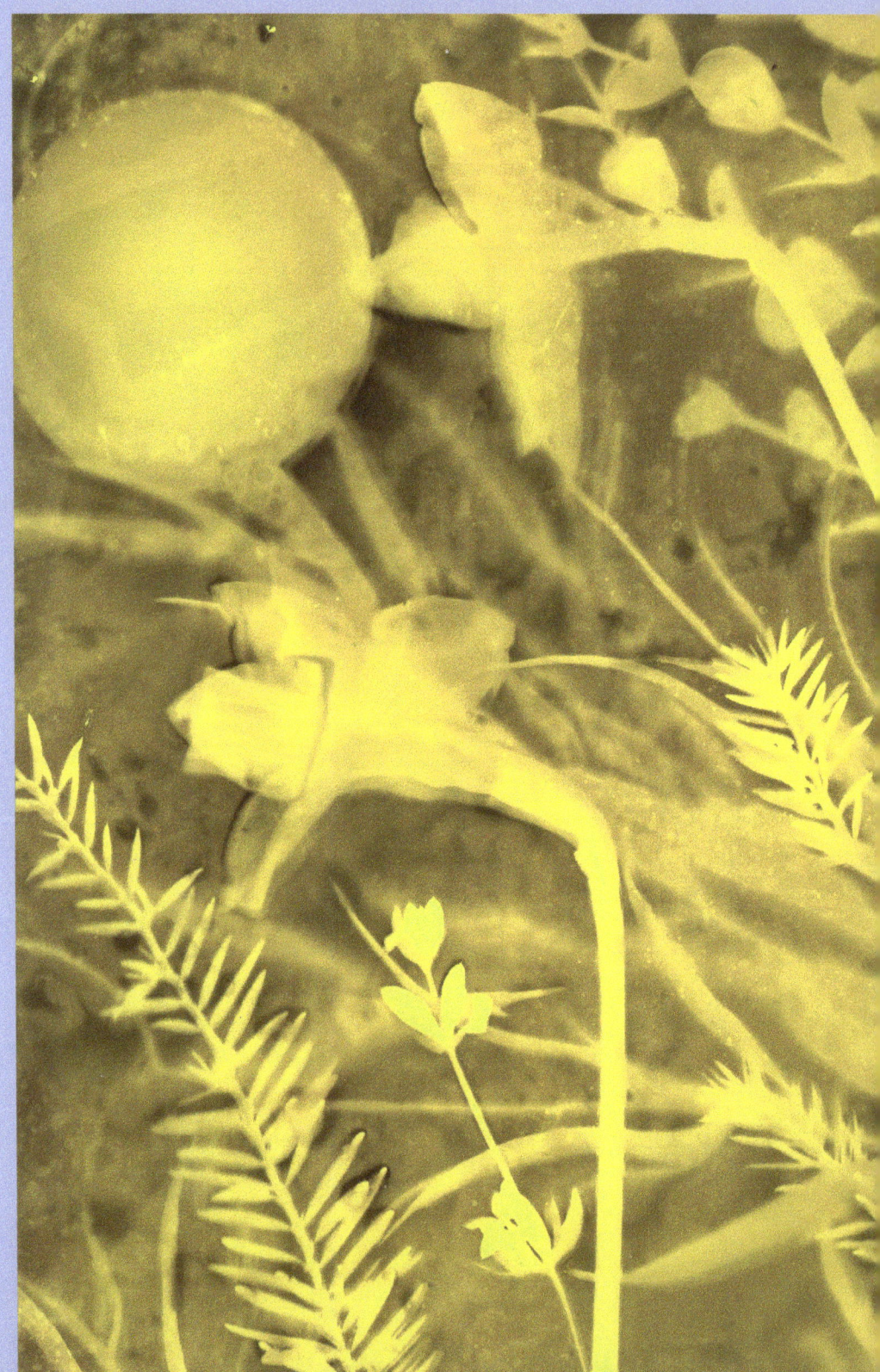

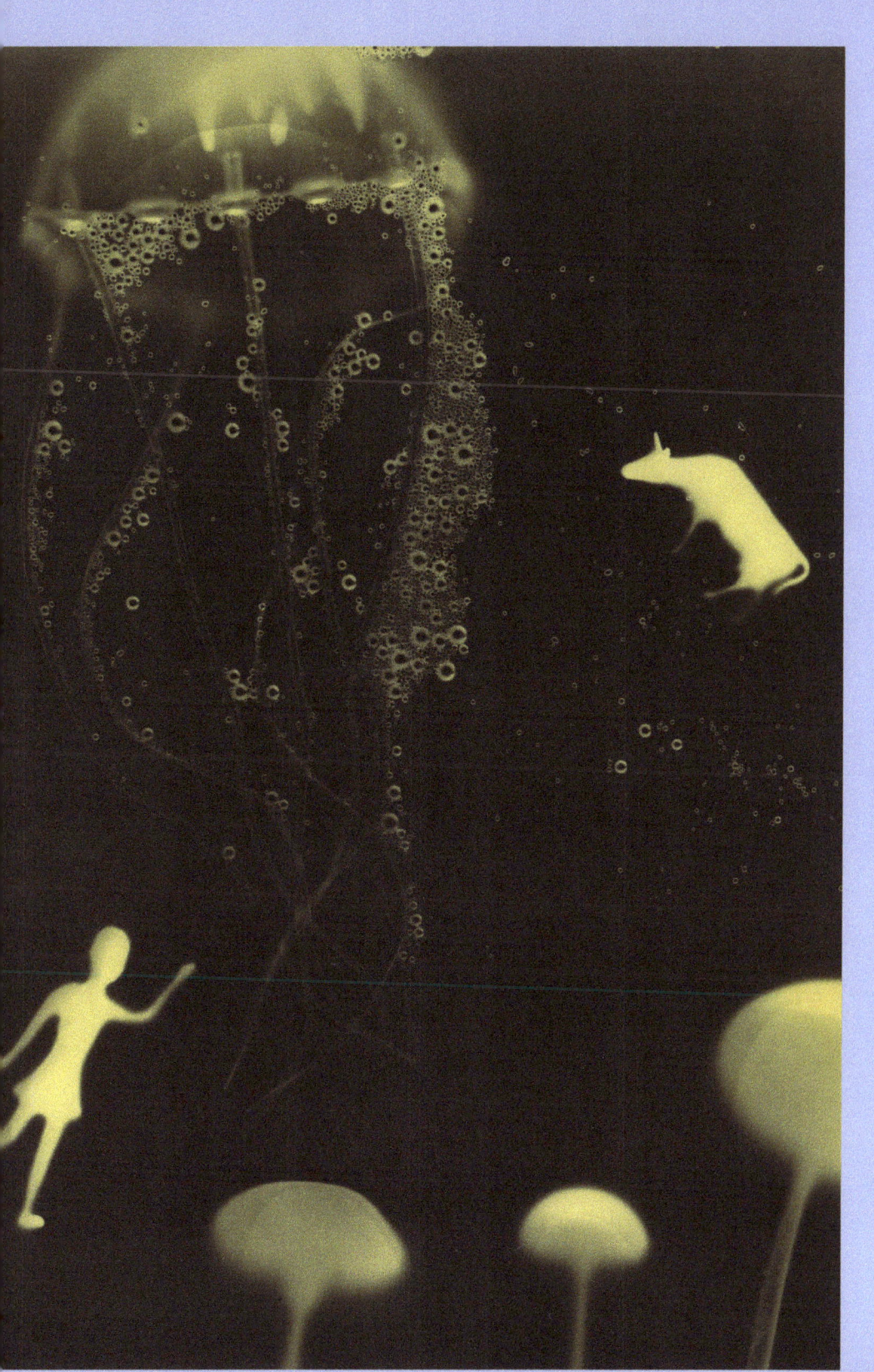

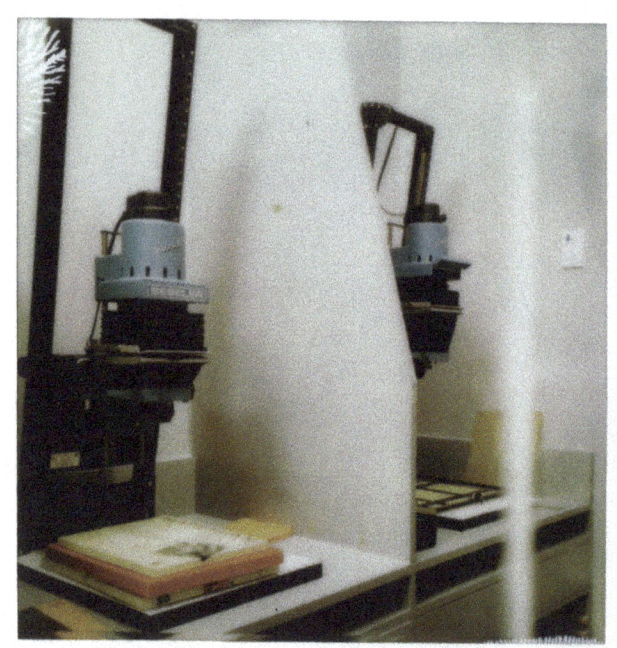

The Halide Project
Philadelphia, PA

ANALOG PASTS AND FUTURES:
PHILADELPHIA AS A CASE STUDY

By Andi Avery

In thinking about the theme of analog futures for this issue, it occurred to me that one of the ways to discern what is wanted and needed for the future is to think about the past. As I type this, I am sitting in my studio in Philadelphia, a city that has an incredibly complicated history with photography, specifically. When we're looking at some of the biggest names in Philly's photographic history, we're looking at art that was funded by historical figures famous for the exploitation of BIPOC folks. This year, we've seen multiple, massive city institutions get called out for exploitative collection and display practices. In a city that is predominantly populated by People of Color, it feels especially important to talk about institutional access for our future. At the moment, Philadelphia's more prominent institutions are taking strides, but largely struggling to meet the moment.

Eadweard Muybridge (you know - the dude with the running horse), conducted many of his motion studies at the University of Pennsylvania right here in the city. The majority of Muybridge's early motion work was financed by Leland Stanford, a robber baron who was infamous for the exploitation of the Chinese immigrants who built the railroad that made him wealthy, as well as the displacement and murder of thousands of Indigenous people during his time as Governor and during the building of Stanford University on Muwekma-Ohlone land [1]. Muybridge and Stanford met and began working together after Stanford retired and took up horse breeding. Stanford paid Muybridge $50,000 (about 1 million dollars today) to prove that for a fraction of a second while running, horses took all four feet off the ground. You know, because he was curious and had $50,000 to spare. Once he and

Stanford parted ways, Muybridge attracted the attention of Philadelphia artist Thomas Eakins, who helped him raise money from Philadelphia's elite to continue his work.

Eakins also created a large portion of his work in Philadelphia - and the city will never let you forget it. Although numerous scholars have written about Eakins's long history of exploitative behavior including sexual violence and misconduct, that seems to have been forgotten (or, more likely, ignored) by the city. We have an Eakins historical marker in the center of our city, the Eakins Oval (a fittingly stressful traffic circle), and the National Register of Historic Places has certified Eakins's old house. In 2006, two Philadelphia institutions and numerous funders, including the Pugh Foundation, scrambled to pull together $68 million to keep Eakins's painting "The Gross Clinic" from leaving the city. Philadelphia's financially insecure artists are relieved, I'm sure.

2021 brought a bit of a reckoning in the art world, here and elsewhere. Eakins's personal archive, which contained many photos of nude minors from whom a record of consent by a guardian was not obtained or available, was previously available on the internet without censorship. Local artist Mary Enoch Elizabeth Baxter, after seeing Eakins's photos of an anonymous, nude prepubescent Black girl in the collection, created her incredibly poignant piece Consecration to Mary in which she inserted images of herself into Eakins's photos as a protective and mothering presence to the subject. In an open letter spearheaded by Baxter, over 200 artists added their names to support her request that Philadelphia's major institutions "formally cease and desist their love affair with Thomas Eakins."

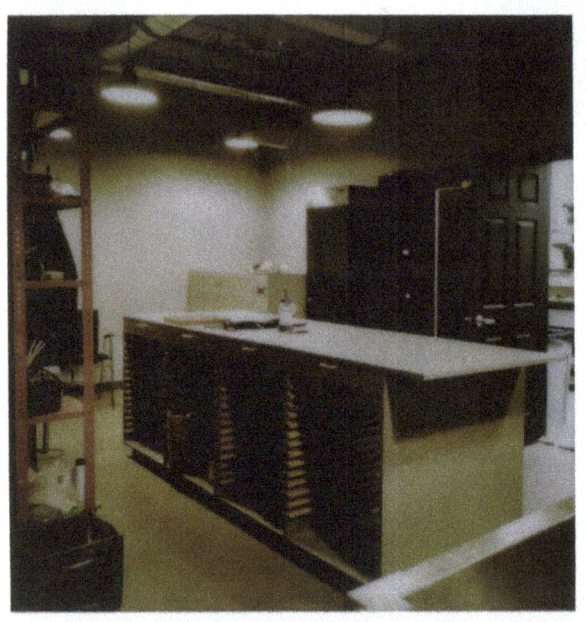

it became clear to me that there are smaller, newer institutions that are setting a thoughtful model for what our relationship to art and photography could be.

Nestled into Philadelphia's Kensington neighborhood exists The Halide Project, Philadelphia's newest non-profit community darkroom that is set to open its doors any day now. I was able to speak with Dale Rio, a wildly talented film photographer and one of THP's founding members, who told me that, "one thing that we like to strive for at Halide is creating a welcoming space." I was able to see the space a week later, and upon taking a tour and meeting a few of the other folks in Halide's orbit, I can say that portion of their goal was indeed successful.

Among other things, the space features a seven-bay B&W gang darkroom with five Omega D5s and two Beseler 23Cs, a film processing area with both steel and plastic tanks for roll film and tanks for sheet film processing, a lovingly-built four-bay UV exposure unit and dedicated coating area for alternative processes, and a private darkroom with Jobo ATL3 unit for color film and print processing. There is also a fairly large gallery space,

Why is it so hard to get Philadelphia's institutions (see also: all institutions, academia, etc.) to acknowledge their own historical bias? The answer is, of course, complicated. Historically, it has been considered objectively good for institutions to collect and store objects. For centuries, artists' work products have been furiously hoarded for collection and display in institutions that weren't necessarily accessible. We consider the digitization of archives and work to be positive from an access perspective, but it's also allowing a lot of work to become public without thought or consideration. It's becoming increasingly obvious that good stewardship of any collection includes not taking a neutral position, because neutrality around objects that used to cause harm leaves space for them to continue to do so.

In thinking about these parts of our past (accessibility, stewardship, education, and community relationships),

which was in transition to a juried show when I stopped by.

One of the things I spoke about with Dale was accessibility, and she was very clear about the fact that the board is in frequent communication around how to equitably accommodate the needs of the community. One of my favorite features of the space was a camera lending library that will be available to all members. The collection is already impressive and still growing. Currently, they are also seeking volunteers, and plan to offer a work-exchange program for darkroom time.

Although the ongoing pandemic dramatically pushed back THP's opening date, they have had, and continue to have, virtual artists talks that occur every other Monday night, and quarterly group critiques available. These events are on a pay-what-you-wish basis, with a suggested donation of $10. The featured speakers include artists from all over the world, and have served an audience just as broad. The featured speakers include artists who work in palladium, cyanotype, pinhole photography, gum bichromate, multiple exposures, and more. Just as The Halide Project has created a dedicated space for an array of historic and alternative processes, so too have they made a digital space for artists working with historic processes.

When I asked who has shown

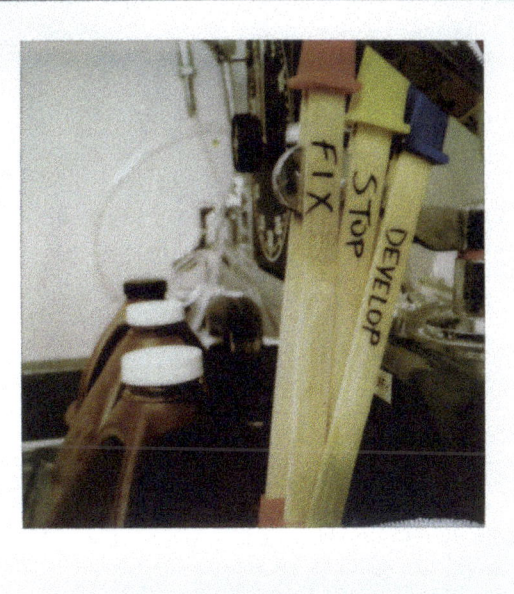

interest so far, Dale told me that a lot of the folks who expressed interest were adults that had access to a darkroom in college and wanted to come back, and younger folks who found their way to a darkroom through digital work. She also mentioned that often, people just want to dive into a new method or build a new workflow. In stark contrast to collecting institutions which often value abundance at whatever cost, The Halide Project seems to be listening to and focusing on artists and their processes, while paying special attention to their specific community needs. "[People] want to slow down," Dale said to me at the conclusion of our interview as we spoke about the resurgence of analog processes and our collective post-pandemic needs, "They want a little bit [of] that slow, meticulous process that film photography or alt-pro has."

Honestly, same.

You can find more about the Halide Project at TheHalideProject.org.

MEMEING THE FUTURE

An

Interview

with

@24MemesPerSecond

By Hogan Seidel & Gabby Sumney

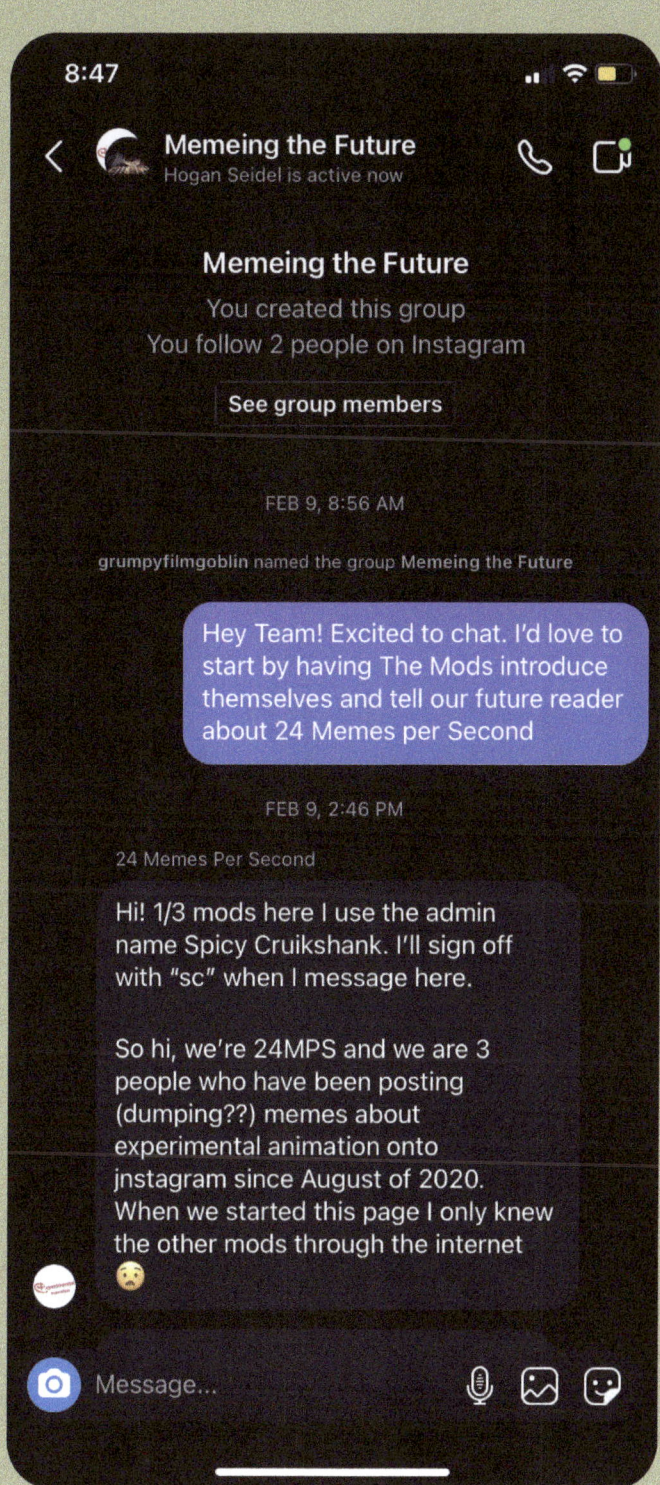

8:47

< **Memeing the Future**
Hogan Seidel is active now

Memeing the Future
You created this group
You follow 2 people on Instagram

See group members

FEB 9, 8:56 AM

grumpyfilmgoblin named the group Memeing the Future

Hey Team! Excited to chat. I'd love to start by having The Mods introduce themselves and tell our future reader about 24 Memes per Second

FEB 9, 2:46 PM

24 Memes Per Second

Hi! 1/3 mods here I use the admin name Spicy Cruikshank. I'll sign off with "sc" when I message here.

So hi, we're 24MPS and we are 3 people who have been posting (dumping??) memes about experimental animation onto jnstagram since August of 2020. When we started this page I only knew the other mods through the internet 😥

Message...

Mod 2/3 hello :)) I go by Helen Chill 🙇 I joined a lil later after sending memes unprompted to the page and wanting in hehe

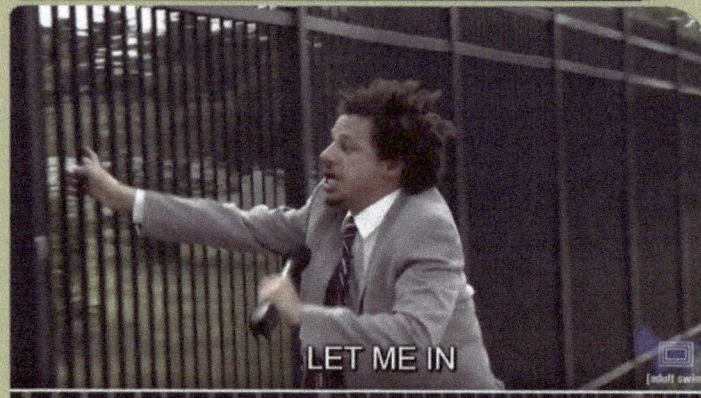

LET ME IN

LET ME INNNNNN!!!

Like the rest of us, I love animation, animators (mostly), and am chronically online whoopsie ! 🙇

Hahah seconding the chronically online part 🙇 but it seems like the internet is the only place to gather as animators in These Times -sc

Hi! Mod 3/3 here, I go by Robert Beer 😎. Spicy and Helen summed it up well. Driven to new online depths in early pandemic times we found ourselves memeing to stay sane. One day we just decided to take it public, and the rest is history!

Beautiful! I do want to say off the bat that roughly 30% of communication between Hogan and me is based on your memes.

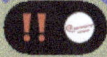

I want to start this discussion of futures with the past. Preservation and historiography, specifically. This page is doing some incredible work connecting people to animation history and to resources for animator regardless of education or career stage. Did you anticipate that you'd be doing that kind of cultural work? How did it evolve from a release valve to my favorite way to learn about experimental animation?

Hahah that's so sweet!! Meme's really are a super-communication device.

This is a great Q. Tbh, at the beginning we had no real expectations. We were really doing it to make ourselves laugh. I think the animation history angle came naturally bcuz we're all just actually nerds about this stuff. Personally, I've always been frustrated by how inaccessible experimental animation is as a field, so making meme's about harder to find/ see films felt like a good way to bridge the gap. -RB

It sometimes overlaps with our own respective practices or interests. I've been doing a bunch of research on queer animation so i've been making gay memes about gay films 😜 - hc

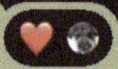

RB is a theory head so I know he makes memes about whatever hes reading too ☃️

I just like looking at history and archive stuff and it's fun to share and see what people have to add to it. Sometimes we pull stuff up as a question like: anyone have more info? It's so fun to just have so many knowledgeable animation people on hand

I was making some anim history memes before 24mps officially started so I guess it was something I was doing to try to talk to make friends online and we just continued that 😳

😣 sc

24memespersecond · · ·

Have you heard of Richard Williams?

No 🖤

24memespersecond Survival who?

Me: i hope the frame rate isnt too high
The frame rate :

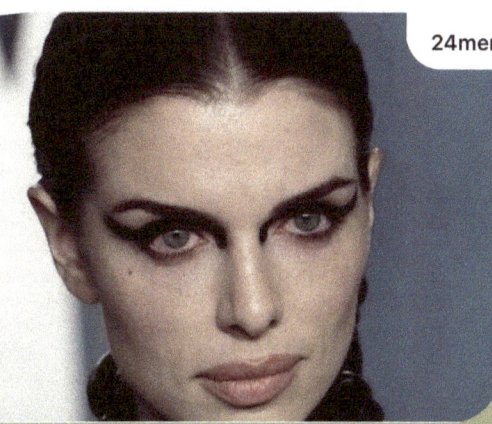

49

Hi hi hi!! Hogan here. Just some random exp film/photo/animation queerdo. Big fan ❤️ 😳 especially of the ~gay~ content..

❤️ 🔘

You have already started to talk about this in terms of your practice(s) connection to your memes, but I was wondering if you see any connections between meme-making and experimental animation? Like conceptually/aesthetically?

For sure. I think meme's work so well bcuz of the relationship between popular imagery/formats and the niche/subversive/comedic content injected into them. Experimental animation historically has worked the same way by utilizing the dominate modes and practices of industry/ mainstream animation but in more personal and exploratory ways. For me, they both represent a democratization of access to an art form and media. - RB

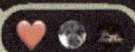

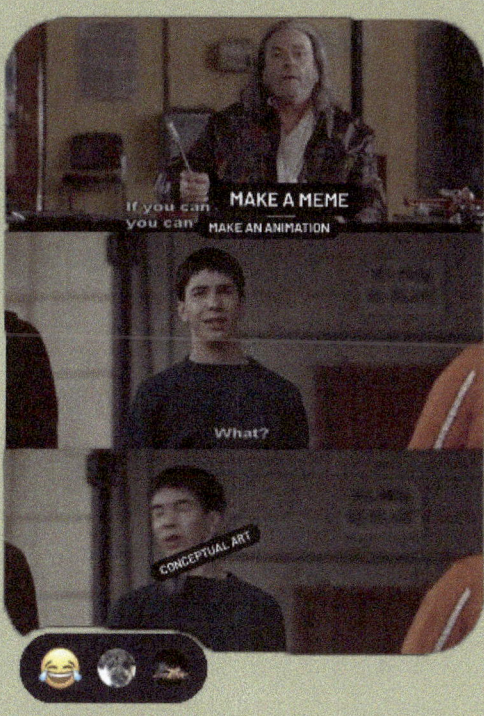

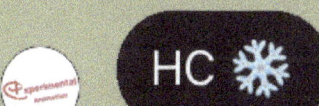

HC ❄️

Some of my favorite approaches to EA involve brevity. Brevity of line, concept, rendering etc. I want immediacy! Brevity is the soul of wit and I'm trying to wrap this up as best I can ❄️

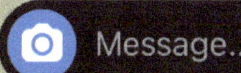

Message...

SALIN

Salin is a short, 3 minutes film. I revisit a family film shot by my grandfather. The images shot in Super 8 in 1966 are masked and revealed by an organic film made from algae.

Formed by visual and sound loops, this work explores organic textures related to images shot in Gaspésie in 1966. My grandfather's nervous camera, combined with his fascination for innocuous movements, resonates with my artistic practice. An organic algae-based film creation workshop offered by TAIS - Toronto Animated Image Society gave me the pretext to play with these images, allowing me to work with film organically and ecologically, but also playfully. Animator Vladimir Konic invented a method to create and digitize a film stock made from algae. The textures and colors created with these organic inks and films grabbed me. Their combination with recently digitized family archive images came about naturally. What could be more natural than combining Gaspésie'lansdcapes with textures of algae? The process combines analog and digital technologies, 8mm film, and organic film. The soundtrack comes from unused audio scraps from other projects.

I think the future of analog film lies in the ecological exploration of the medium, either through plant-based developers for processing or by recycling material as found footage. Combining film with other materials and digital technologies, sharing our knowledge and experiments, that's what helps to keep it available and alive.

ANNE-MARIE BOUCHARD

What inspired Salin?

I created Salin d out of a need to play
and experiment. I made it as part
of ongoing research on sustainable
practices and processes in filmmaking.

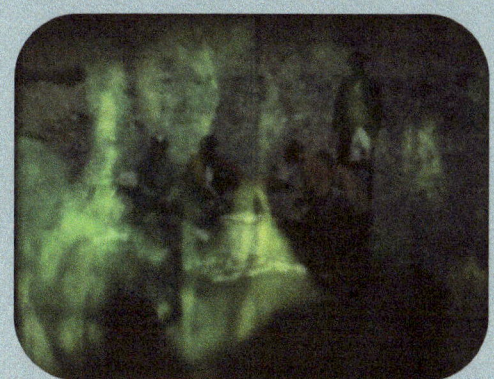

The Super 8mm footage used in this
film comes from family footage. The
pictures I chose for this film are the
first I remember seeing projected.
They were my first contact with home
movies and the magic of the projected
light when I was 5 or 6 years old.
Most of the family was uninterested
in these seagulls, but I remember
being fascinated. They are somewhat
banal images, yet they keep trace of
a specific moment in time. They bring
back the memory of the people who
disappeared since their filming.
I can relate to my grandfather filming
the seagulls: it is the sort of thing I
would capture when on holiday. Is it
because these films I saw at an early
age influenced my way of looking
at things, even before I could hold a
camera?

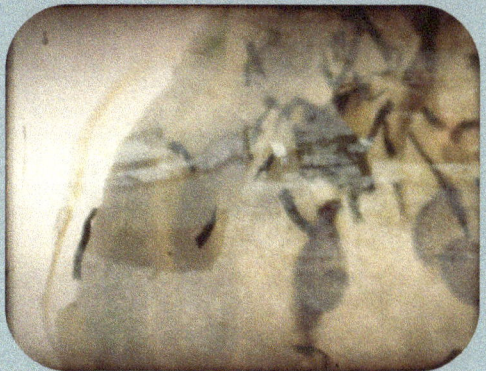

I got interested in organic filmstock:
a homemade film base made entirely
of cheap, organic, biodegradable
material. An animation workshop
allowed me to experiment with
fabricating such a material.

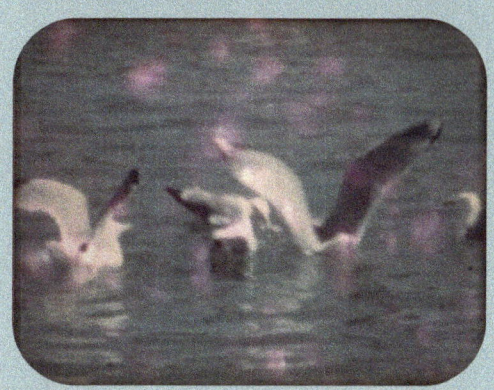

Somehow, the two collided: images of
a trip to the sea and algae-based film
stock. They just blended so perfectly! I
just had the Super8 film scanned not
too long before the workshop, so the
images were fresh in my mind, with a
lingering desire to do something with

them. I like that form and content respond to one another so well, a bit like a mirror effect, but one that is a little bit distorted, so you see something different than was is there.

Tell us about your algae process.

Film animator Vladimir Konic invented this algae process during the first lock-down. Last summer, he gave an online workshop at TAIS (Toronto Animated Image Society). The idea is to create a plant-based film stock to replace celluloid. And to eventually run it through a projector, live.

This process has four steps.

1: Boil the algae (or plants) until translucent. Some vegetables or plants never become translucent; corn leaves turn a pale yellow; berries keep their colours but make great tints.

2: Take the liquid you used for boiling the algae. Mix it with some guar gum or agar-agar until it forms a paste.

3: Place your boiled algae on a baking sheet, in the length and form of a film strip, in a thin layer. Cover with the thickened liquid using a spatula.

4: Dry – in an oven at the lowest temperature for 2-3 hours, plus 2-3 days in a dry place can be necessary for complete dryness. Ready when dry!

I enjoyed this process and started experimenting with different plants since I made Salin. I have some very different organic film stock to experiment with for my future films! White or pale plants work best. Corn leaves stay coloured, but the textures are great.

The result is a bit like homemade translucent paper. It is like a negative film: the light has to shine through it to come alive. And to be used as film, it needs to be scanned. As such, it cannot be projected yet.

It is possible to tint it, sparkle it with seasonings while wet, draw on it or glue over it when dry, to add even more textures to this translucent material.

The next step is to find a way to keep this film stock supple; as it dries, it becomes fragile and breakable. I will try to achieve that by adding another sort of algae or maybe sap from asclépiade leaves or another natural latex. That way, it could be used directly into the projector once one has pierced sprocket holes. We are very far from a usable film base yet!

How did you scan film affected by algae?

I placed the algae stock on a light table and took macro pictures. Since each organic strip is about a foot long, I had about 10 to 12 frames for each strip. I reconstructed the film strip in the computer and transposed it to 16mm (so I had more pictures for each piece to make 24 frames a second). I worked quite some time alternating between Photoshop and After Effects until the result was pleasing,

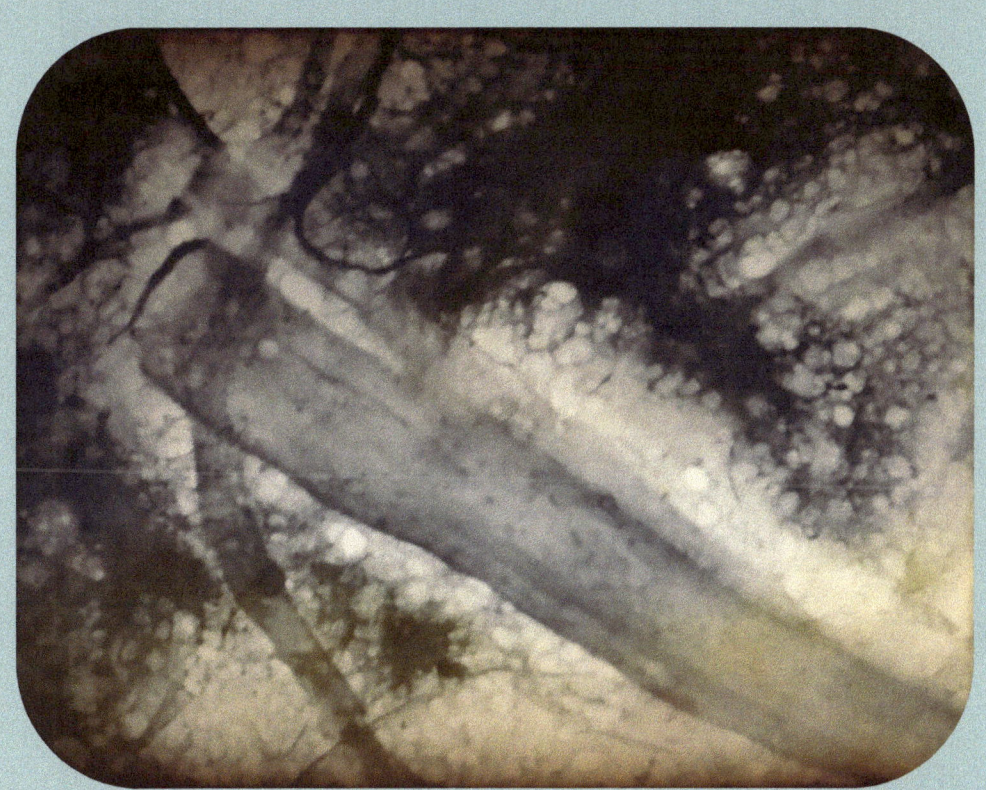

both in terms of speed and size adjustment.

I composited the 8mm footage in After Effects into the algae textures.

I do not own the family film; my aunt treasures it. I would not dare alter it! My aunt still has the working projector, and she still watches these reels of film from time to time. I would never want to deprive her of that. I had it scanned, however, as the film is getting very fragile over time. Since there is only one copy, the scan made it accessible for the entire family. I can now play with the digital scan without damaging the family memories/ archives.

My film is a mixture of analogue, organic and digital film. They all blend to make the images. I think it makes sense on many levels. The processes mingle, intertwine, become intimately connected. Every project I made on analogue film was scanned and edited with digital software. The combination of digital and analog technologies allows the analogue processes to gain a great deal of accessibility. Steinbeck's are hard to come by. The nearest optical printer is 350 km away. And this film, in particular, emphasizes the relationship between time and progress: images from the 60s shot on what was then consumer level media, worked digitally with tools available to most, envisioning a sustainable way to make movies that is yet to be perfected.

Throughout the film, we hear running water and what sounds like bells. How did you create the soundscape?

The first sound I thought of for this piece is the music of the sea. I had a few recordings of the waves hitting the beach in Rimouski, on the

St-Lawrence River. I find them calming and soothing. They are the sound of holidays, of rest, of contact with nature.

I also used a recording I made with musician and friend Lyne Goulet. It was recorded for another project but never used. Lyne was playing a tune by hitting wine glasses with a spoon. I used it to bring rhythm. They sound eerie and echo-ey. To me, these sounds bring both nostalgia and unease. They are punctuations in the waves.

Lyne also played some engaging chimes sounds. They are higher-pitched, so they lift the spirits a bit. I associate it with dreams, early memories.

I like to work with field recordings. Their sound is not perfect; it is closer to real life. I remember the feeling of what happened at the moment of the recording. I get attached to sounds.

I also like to re-use and revisit sounds I recorded for different purposes. They form a soundscape from which I pluck and pick, where my ears remember a sound when silent images play. I then play trial and error while associating the sounds and the pictures until they fit. Sometimes I change the sequence a bit, sometimes the sounds. I travel a lot from one to the other.

What keeps you going as a filmmaker? Do you have any mentors or work with any labs?

Film festivals keep me going. I have not travelled much for the last couple of pandemic years, and I find I miss those in-person gatherings. I enjoyed the virtual Q&A and filmmakers' meetings the past two years, and though it is not quite the same as gathering in festivals, it was nice to meet and exchange around experimental processes and film. I can rarely afford to go abroad, and these virtual meetings allowed me to be there.

I am inspired by Pierre Hébert, Stephen Woloshen, and of course, Norman McLaren. I also am emulated by Sarah Seené and Guillaume Vallée's work.

I am interested in eco-processing and sustainable alternative analog processes. I am taking workshops here and there, greatly facilitated by the pandemic: many artist-run centers offer online, not too expansive workshops. It is necessary to question my practice, to come across new ideas and new experiments. These workshops are there for that purpose. This is why I got interested in the Vladimir Konic workshop.
This continual experimentation & exploration also keep me going! I enjoy seeing what happens to the pictures and sounds when I transform them, either chemically or digitally.

I usually work with Niagara Custom Lab or Main Film when I need a film scan.

What themes recur in your artwork? Do you feel like there's been any throughline that you haven't/can't/won't abandon?

Film is about time: stopping it, slowing it, fast-forwarding it, keeping moments intact and going back to them indefinitely. I cannot help being fascinated with that. And the way we see things differently when time goes by; something beautiful becomes something sad, sometimes. Simple gestures become traces of what was, once, and is no longer.
I feel my films are about loss, in relationship with time: loss of youth, loss of memory, loss of dear people. Even though I do not film people - I film mostly nature- my films are about people: being human, fragile and submitted to time.

I am attracted by working directly with the matter, the physicality of the analogue film itself. I like to see the image transformed, becoming abstract. The picture is dying but becoming another, revealing some secret. There is a search for enlightenment in my filmmaking.

Enlightenment in the sense of trying to see through the surface of the image, to see the light underneath it that made it possible. It is a metaphor for my search for understanding – or a purpose. It is my way of coping with living, I guess.

What's next for you?

I am working on La dissolution du paysage, a short animated experimental 16mm film. I draw and etch animations direct on film. I also chemically alter the film by boiling it, ironing it, adding vinegar, salt, soap, rust, etc.
My film will be about loss and metamorphosis, memory and fear.
I am working with musicians, attempting to create the music together with the images. But it is quite a challenge, as it takes me a long time to make my animations on film, and the music is evolving faster than I can draw. We go back and forth, putting our ideas together.

I also work on plant-based film processing during a darkroom residency. I look forward to that. I will try out recipes, experimenting with temperatures and duration until I come up with a formula that works for me. I will experiment with eco-reversal film processing, to project my film directly, for performances, for example. And I will also research sustainable ways to deal with the chemical by-products of the lab. So, I have a big agenda!

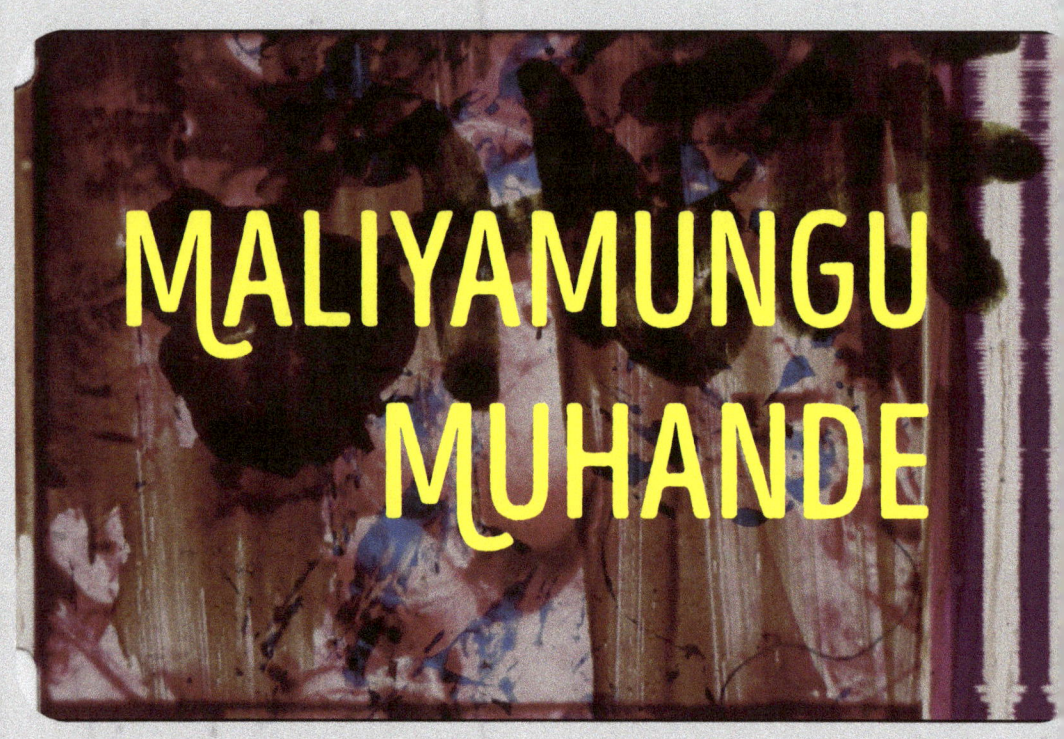

MALIYAMUNGU MUHANDE

CAMERALESS FOUND FOOTAGE FILM

ALIVE IN DEATH

Tell us about *Alive in Death*. What inspired this film?

Alive in Death is an experimental film made with 60 millimeter found footage. The film is an exploration of a trauma I lived through, and an investigation of what engaging, as a black person, with 60 millimeter film—grappling with the problematic pasts of the medium, of the form—might mean.

On July 5, 2018, I was in a gas explosion where I nearly lost my life. I'm still processing the event, and I've been unsure about how exactly to process it through art. When I had the idea of destroying film—bending, burning, scratching the film—it felt like a liberation from the preciousness of handling film. A subversion of film. I took that opportunity to go somewhere dark.

I also saw it as an opportunity to allow myself to dive further into the idea of decolonizing film. How can I say that filmmaking is healing for me when in fact it's also caused so much damage to the way I see myself as a black woman? From an early age, media capped my ability to imagine because I never saw myself in those representations. It was saying, You're not enough, you're not worthy to be seen, you can't do this. You can only do as much as you can see, right? What I could see was a world constructed around the ideas, the manipulation, the dictation, that blackness is inferior to whiteness.

And so what inspired Alive in Death is inquiry and curiosity, and seeking healing from trauma. The question I asked myself is, What could it look like to step outside of film-making norms and recreate—reuse, remake—something for myself, as a black woman filmmaker today?

How did you collect footage for this film?

The footage came from my professor, Melissa Freedling, who is my experimental 60 millimeter documentary film godmother. She offered me found footage that she had collected and wasn't using—that she had, in this way, curated for me to have. And I remember precisely that part of the concept matched my desire to find resonance in other people's "secondhand" property. You know, the idea of film being something that was created for white people by white people. It was about allowing the process of collection, of manipulation and animation, to reflect that fact, that truth—and subverting it.

The primary focus for me was to allow myself to go back to the gas explosion, allow myself to go back to the event through the 60 millimeter found footage, and try to find connection between what I was recollecting from the traumatic event and what I was seeing on film. To allow the 60 millimeter film to sort of be my imaginary friend and accompany me through the accident.

So the image of the dog allowed a bit of dissociation as I was recollecting the event. I could dissociate and visualize instead

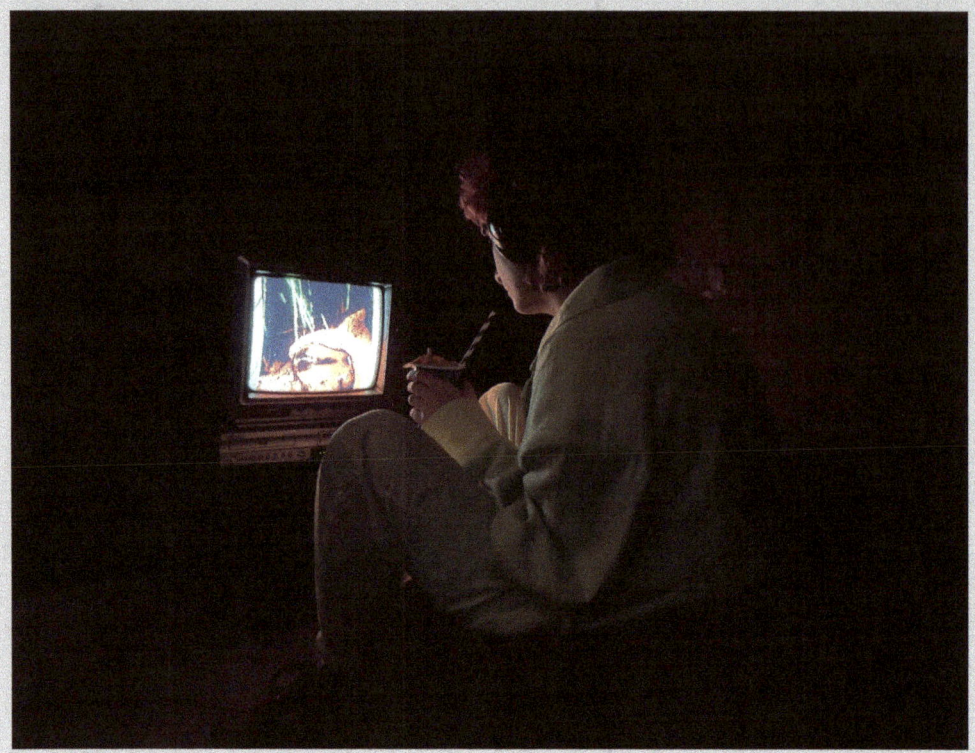

of thinking of myself actually in the gas explosion, which felt too close—instead, putting those attributes to the dog, putting those attributes to the fish. And later, putting the attributes of white supremacist negligence, the oppressive forces that kept the gas explosion quiet, attributing that to the white man with the microscope who showed up in the film, to my surprise.

It was a process of allowing these found images to help me think back on the accident, then bringing that a step further to consider how I could subvert this footage and apply my own traumatic event to reclaim the film's content, to reimagine what this complete form—finished film—could be made into, in spaces of decolonization. I wanted to take us out of the colonial world and into an expansion of decolonial practices, innovation

and rethinking. It was very much a process of allowing myself to work from a place of the unknown.

In the film we hear the narrator say The film is burned into scars that resembles the textures of my own scars. How do you view the relationship between film, body, and spirit?

Film has the power to bring us closer to our bodies—in the way we see ourselves and the way we are able to engage with our physical forms—and equally it has the power to distance ourselves from our bodies. It's a powerful tool, with the ability to uplift our spirit or to oppress our spirits. I can't answer the question without acknowledging the history of film, that it was created for whiteness. As in, the techne, the technology itself, was built to see and capture white people and not black people. So with that information, I can say that there's a relationship between film, my body, and my spirit. Because prior to my decolonial inquiry and practice and growth within this medium, the connection between film, my body, and my spirit was to further myself from my real identity. Until I started unlearning and I started to learn how to love myself.

On another level, in this film the relationship between film and my body is made literal. The narrator is me, and the process of creating the burns on film was spiritually healing to me. I used heated metal to press down on the 60 millimeter film. And anybody who's worked with fire on film has experienced, you know, it's not an easy scrape to make. You have to sort of press down and scrape off. And that's basically the same thing that has to happen when your skin is badly burnt. The first layer of skin that's burnt needs to be scraped off. So it was basically reenacting that process, that I have experienced with my own body, to find healing from it. I close my eyes and if I want to feel it, I can feel it, right now, I can feel the pain.

Film is a powerful physical and spiritual tool, and it's important for us to acknowledge its past–and to some degree, its present–and to engage in the form, the medium, the content, in a subversive way to inquire and to build a better world. A better cinematic world, a better film world, a better world.

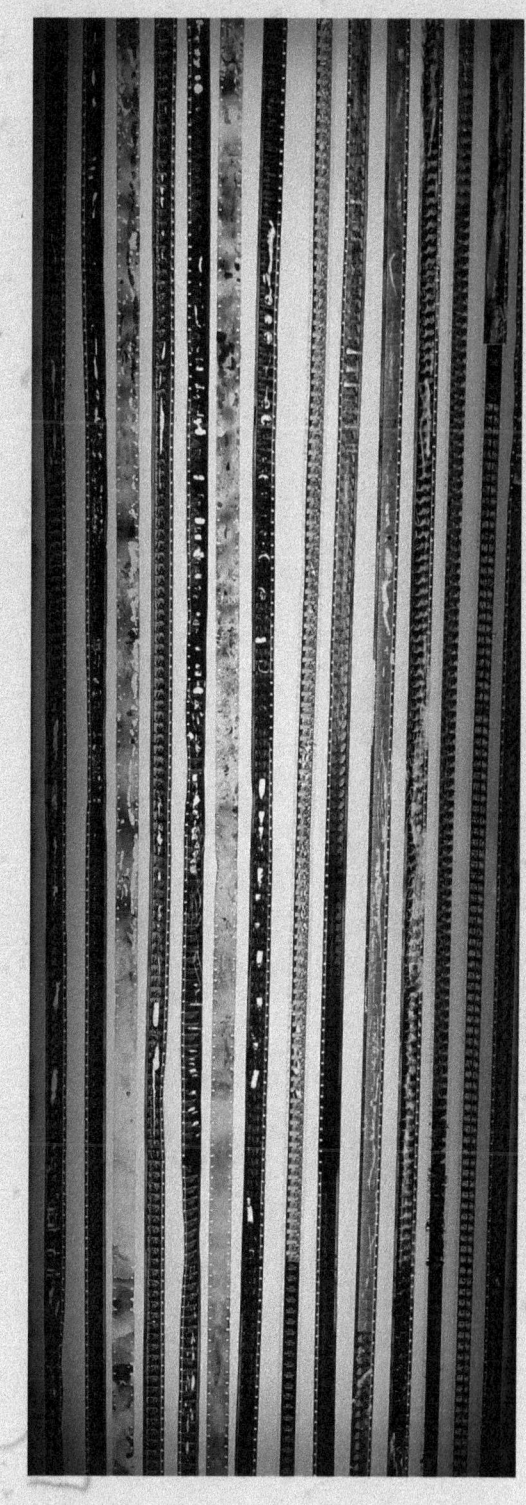

OPALINE

A childhood memory as the nodal point of a disturbed life; a disappearance leaving an indelible mark on the retina; a cumbersome experience that must be exorcised. This is the start of this experimental short film. Beyond the memory of childhood, it is the subjects of objectification and hypotonic immobility that are addressed.

The images that make up this video poem, were originally captured by the camera, filmed with a Super 8 camera, developed by hand, and then painted. The painting that runs over the film thus rehabilitates the movement in a frozen and anxious daily life.

Opaline was made while in a mentorship program with Vidéographe in Montreal under the mentor Guillaume Vallée.

ALIX GALDIN

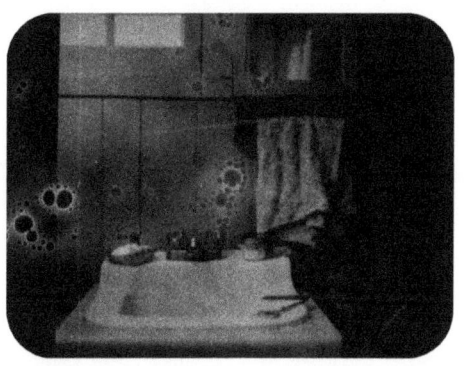
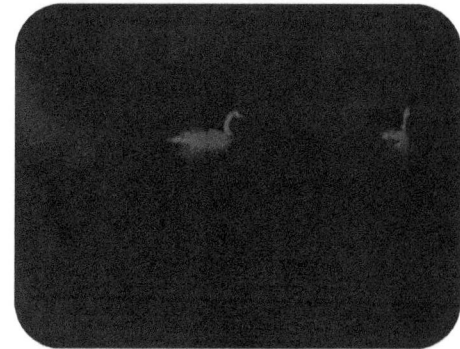
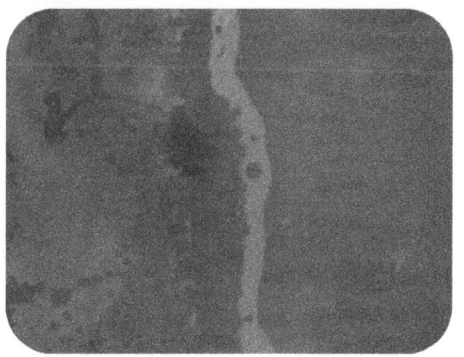
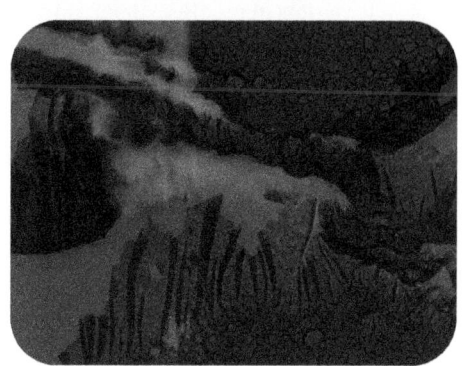

What inspired Opaline?

First, what led me to make this film was the exploration of a childhood memory. I was a victim of a certain form of violence due to the alcoholism of one of my parents, and I tried to understand what crystallized in this precise memory, which haunts me in my adult life. So, I wrote an autofictional text in 2018, which I wanted to put into images afterwards.

In a second step, I questioned myself on the notion of objectification through this memory. Like many girls, I was a victim of sexual harassment and abuse as a teenager. It took me time and resources to understand and accept this. Concerned by this violence, I explored the feelings related to the state of immobility of a victim caused by an aggression.

More generally, I believe that sexual harassment and abuse suffered in childhood are systemic violence that condition us to accept being dominated in adulthood, because they make us integrate an inferiority, especially as a woman. It was necessary for me to address this issue because the more the years go by, the more these abuses are brought to light in my circle of family and friends. I think that talking about it collectively will allow us to find solutions to better address these issues.

Women are particularly victim of this violence but men too. I did not want to neglect this in the film. In French, the protagonist of the text is not gendered, it is a thing, an objectified person. So, it could be a man or a woman. It is difficult to translate this in English.

Tell us about the mentorship program with Vidéographe you're a part of.

The mentorship program is a support offered by the artist-run center Vidéographe in Montreal, which selects four projects per year.

Is designed to encourage the professional and artistic development of early-stage artists by helping them to develop a new project, to explore a new technique, or to continue to produce a work in progress. Thanks to this program, we benefit from sixteen hours of meeting with a professional artist in our field and $1000 in material support. This program is a great opportunity for me and a first recognition as a filmmaker. The person who supports me in this project is Guillaume Vallée, a Quebec experimental filmmaker and video artist, working mainly on Super8, 16mm and VHS.

What's a favorite new technique you've learned as part of the mentorship program?

What inspired me the most was not a technique but rather a tool. I loved using the 16mm JK optical printer, which allows you to do special effects. It's a rare machine that not many people use, but the artist-run center Main Film in Montreal has one and offers courses to learn how to use it.
For this project, Guillaume Vallée showed me how to blow up Super 8 film to 16mm film. This allowed me to make a copy of the original film and then paint directly on the 16mm film. With the optical printer, I was also able to create a variety of effects including slow motion, reverse direction, and split screen. I would like to explore its possibilities and plan to use it for a future film project.
To get an idea of what is possible with the optical printer, I recommend watching the amazing Guillaume Vallée's film Monsieur Jean-Claude.

What do you hope audiences walk away feeling after watching Opaline?

I hope it will make people question what objectification is, and how it affects girls in their adult lives.
I think that art helps to lift taboos and that it allows to approach reality in a more bearable way. I didn't want to water down the subject but rather make it accessible. I hope that the form of the film will facilitate the access.

When and where can we see the finished piece?

I don't know yet when it will be possible to see the finished work, but I hope to present it in festivals next year.

What keeps you motivated/producing?

I think it is vital for me to express myself through the film and photography. I have extreme difficulty to express myself orally,

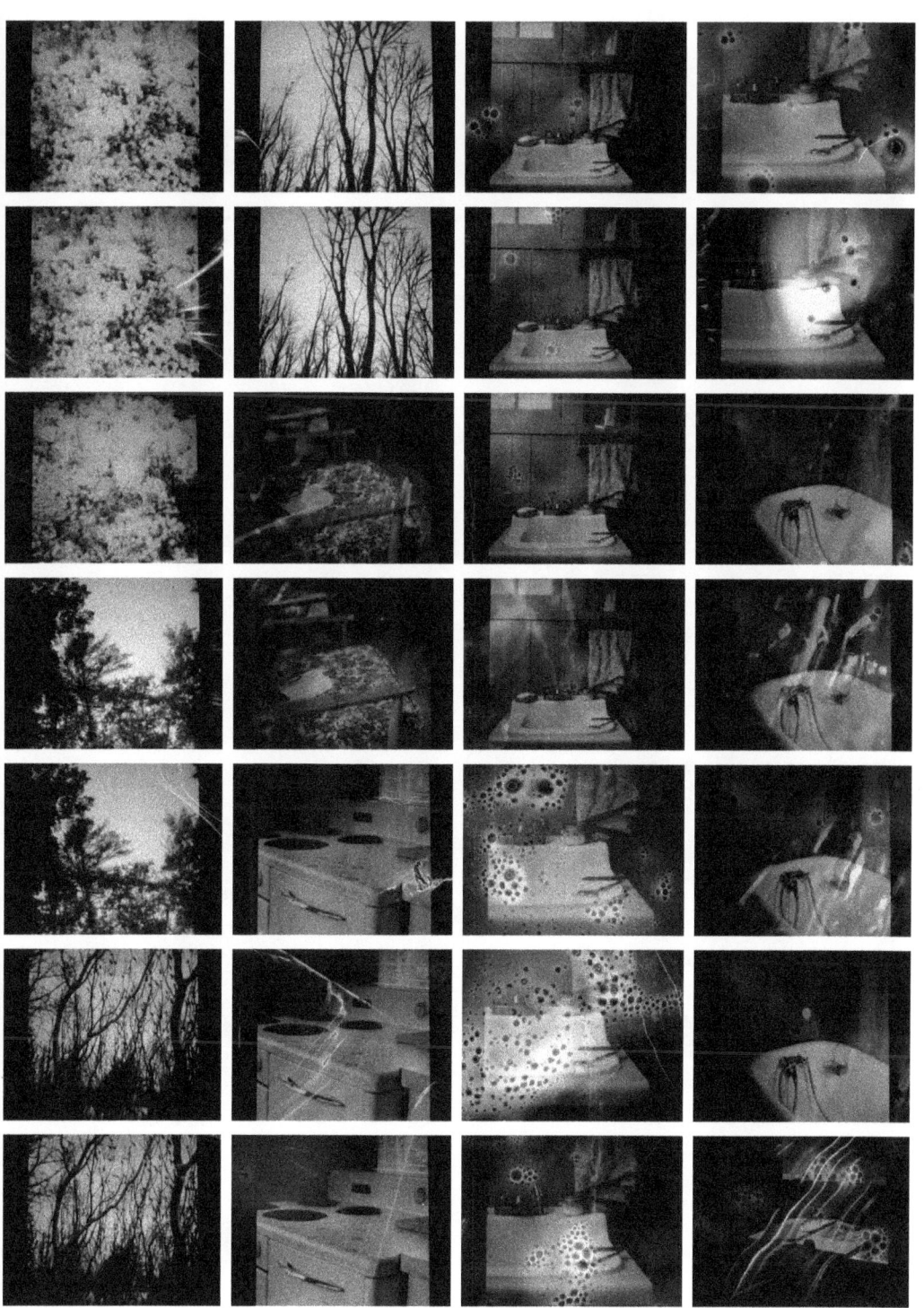

Images taken from work on the film Opaline, selected by Vidéographe as part of the 2021-2022 annual mentorship program. Painting on Super 8mm film

especially in public. The image is a privileged means of communication for me. I feel closer to reality when I express myself in images rather than in words.

Moreover, I find in analogical work a privileged connection with the medium that continually inspires me. I am fascinated by both the technique and the physicality of film. The more I discover the more I want to continue.

It's inspiring to see what has already been experimented with the material of film and the vivid imaginations of filmmakers since cinema has existed. There is so much to learn.

How do we break down barriers for more people to access analog technology?

Maybe by proposing this kind of zine which gives access to a lot of works and methods of creation.

Artists also need to have opportunities to share their skills, in workshops for example. But if we don't want it to be a niche experience, we must be able to reach out to a diverse range of people and get out of dedicated organizations.

It's great to see that there are still some community darkrooms in Quebec.

For 5 years, I was part of a photo club in Montreal that offers courses to a large audience and sometimes works with people with disabilities. With a friend, we had set up a course that gives the opportunity to digital photographers and analog photographers to work together. It went well, and it gave some people the desire to discover the work in darkroom. So maybe breaking down the barriers between practices is a good way of breaking down preconceptions about analog work.

What technique do you use to paint film?

I used water-based glass paint, and Winsor & Newton drawing inks with classic brushes and a sponge pad. The glass paint is more translucent while the ink offers more vivid colors. During the film, the progression in time goes from paint to ink, as I wanted to intensify the colors.

To apply the paint to the film, I cut it into several sections and placed these pieces on a backlit table. Once the strips were painted and dry, I taped them back together.

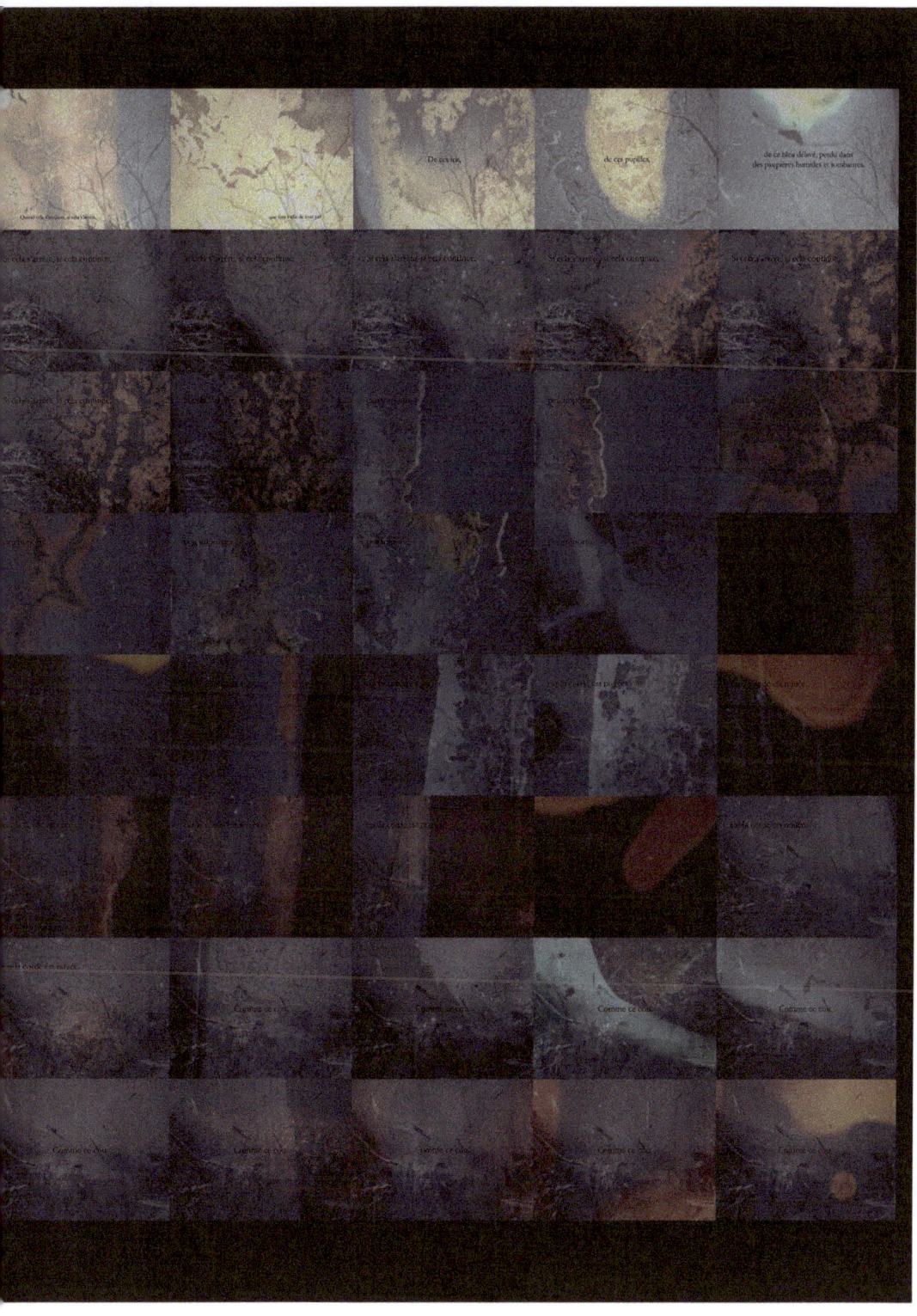

GABRIEL

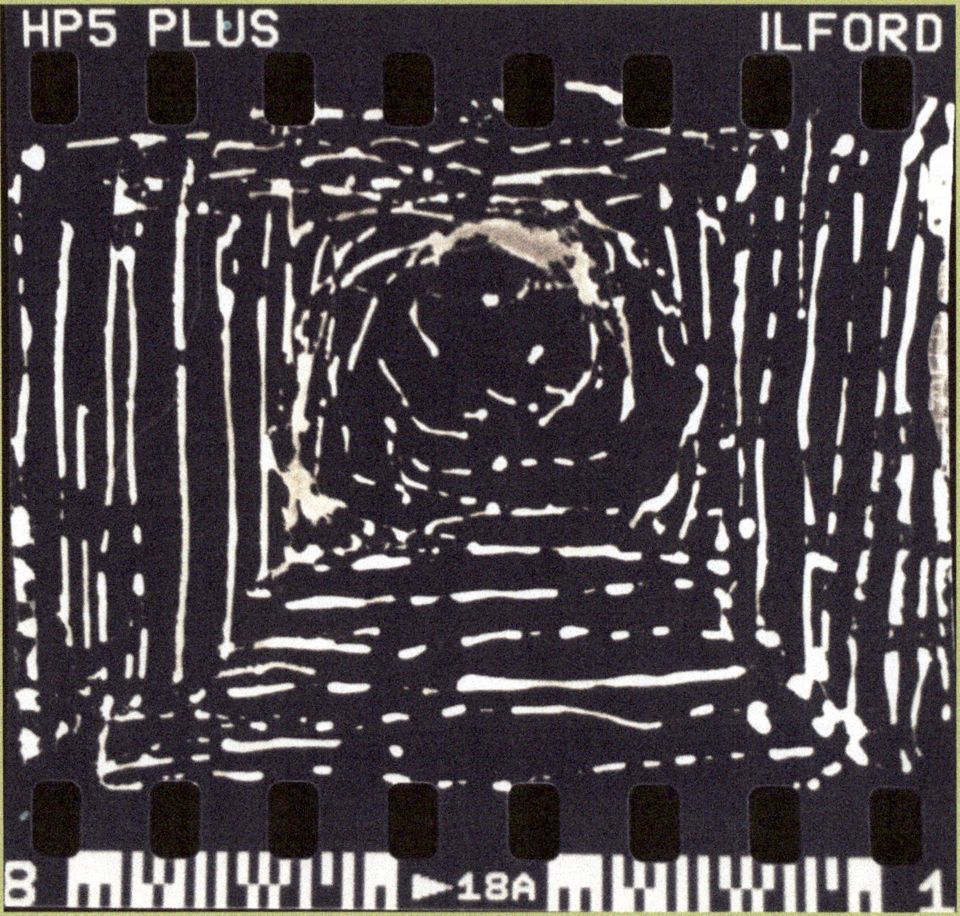

HP5 PLUS   ILFORD

8 ►18A   1

BRYANT

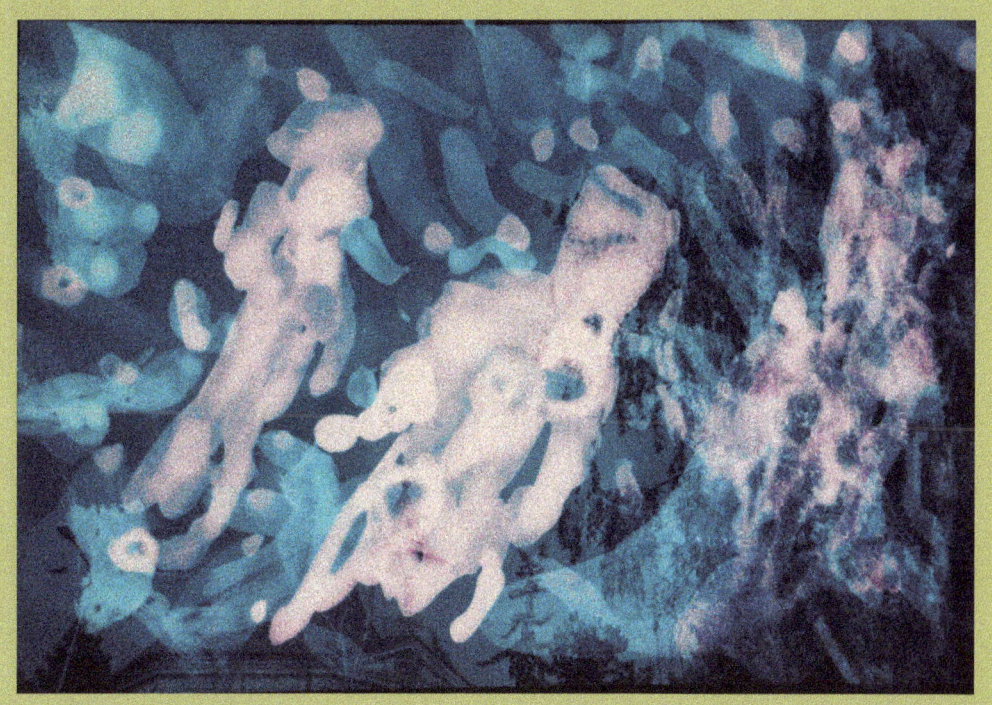

" I started creating daily 'reactive' experiments in response to research made in my dissertation that looked at how the Japanese concept of 'Ma' is used as a form of audio visual manipulation, and how this affects pacing. I ended up creating three films as a response to a major university project. An experimental animation that was the 'Outcomes' of the experiments. A 'Process Film' that looked at the process of making and the third film looking at the outcomes and process in the form of a book.   The first experiments I made were destroying some of my old celluloid film and drawing upon them as frames."

You mention the Japanese concept of Ma. Can you give us a quick rundown of what that means to you and how it applies to your work?

From what I understand, Ma is the Japanese concept that considers the importance of negative space within space and time. Separation is needed to enhance or open up an interpretation. A helpful view of Ma by Issac Stern refers to it as 'the silence between the notes that creates music'

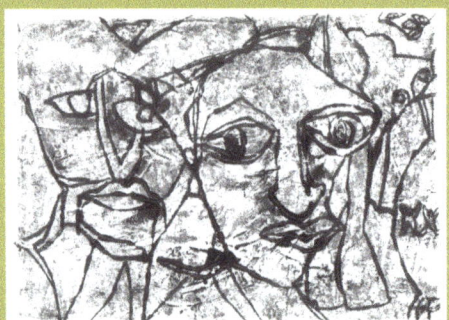

For me, Ma has become an important way to approach the balance between audio and visual communication. This balance separates, abstracts, removes, and also levels out in harmony. Untitled Outcomes is an experiment that explores this balance through reactive making and the audiovisual manipulation of pacing through documentation.

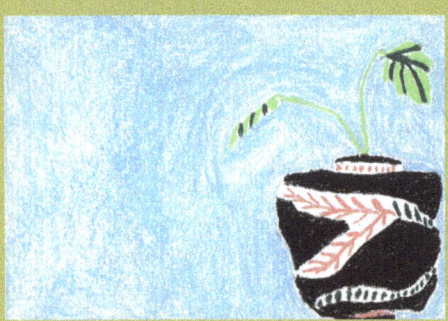

Would you share a few of the processes that you used to manipulate your film? Did you have a favorite or least favorite?

I used some 35mm shots of mine presenting sentimental areas and objects. I then cut them all into individual frames. I was fascinated by the unique and uncontrolled marks that were left behind by 'destroying' the film. Some were boiled and then burnt, others were dashed through a bucket of bleach and left to soak in lemon juice. The remaining, I left in washing-up liquid and coffee. I really enjoyed the immediacy of change that bleach would have. Whereas, burning the film seemed to tighten the image which I was less excited about.

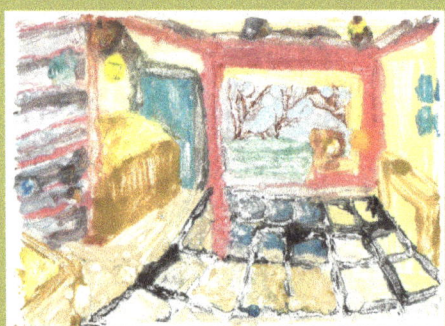

I followed the processes of destroying film with hand-drawn watercolor marks and removing film in the process of scratching the surface with a scalpel.

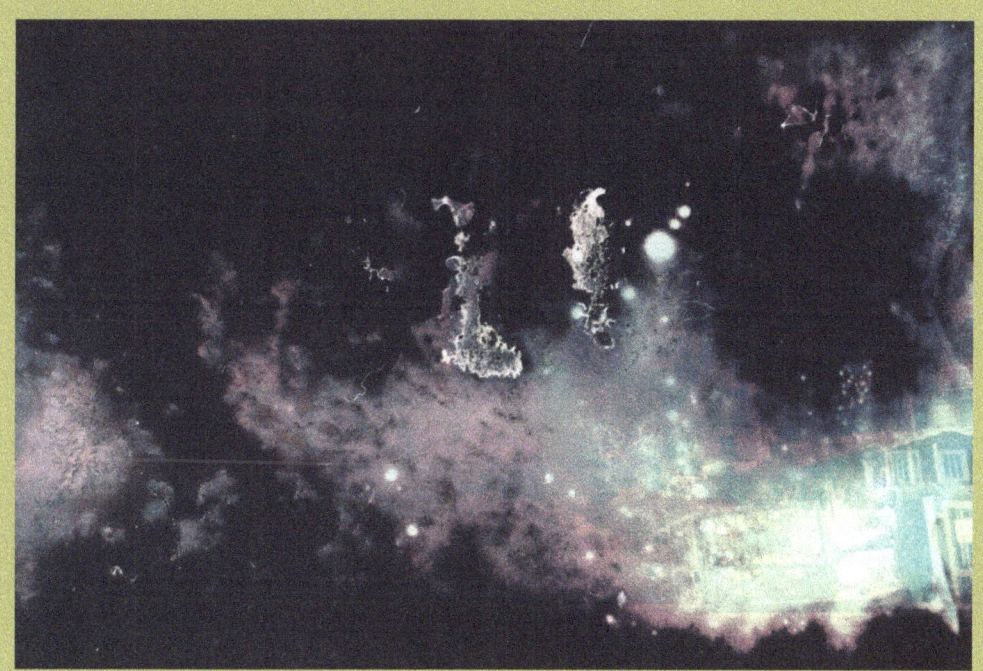

It seems as though the process is just as, if not more important than, the outcome in this case.

The process of making directly influenced what the outcome would be in terms of the materials being used and the actions involved. This meant that the outcomes were separate and also didn't influence each other. It was interesting seeing these outcomes together on a timeline in terms of their placement and how they worked or didn't work together.

Can you tell us how you feel when you are working? And then how do you hope someone would feel looking at it (if anything)?

Being present, unfiltered, and honest has always been an important catalyst for how I would approach making. This unapologetic response to making is very direct and often

comes out of nowhere. The lack of planning helps me to jump straight in, and within the process, find different routes of thought to stumble upon. I would like my viewer to feel confused and disrupted at first. Within this, I would hope that whoever is viewing my work can piece together their own, personal, narratives from what they are seeing and hopefully feel involved along the way.

You mention the term "reactive making," what does this mean?

Reactive making is essentially reacting to a thought, theme, or word through making. It is initially absent of any narrative or direct meaning. Once a visual has been formed this can be repeated but now based upon the previous visual made.

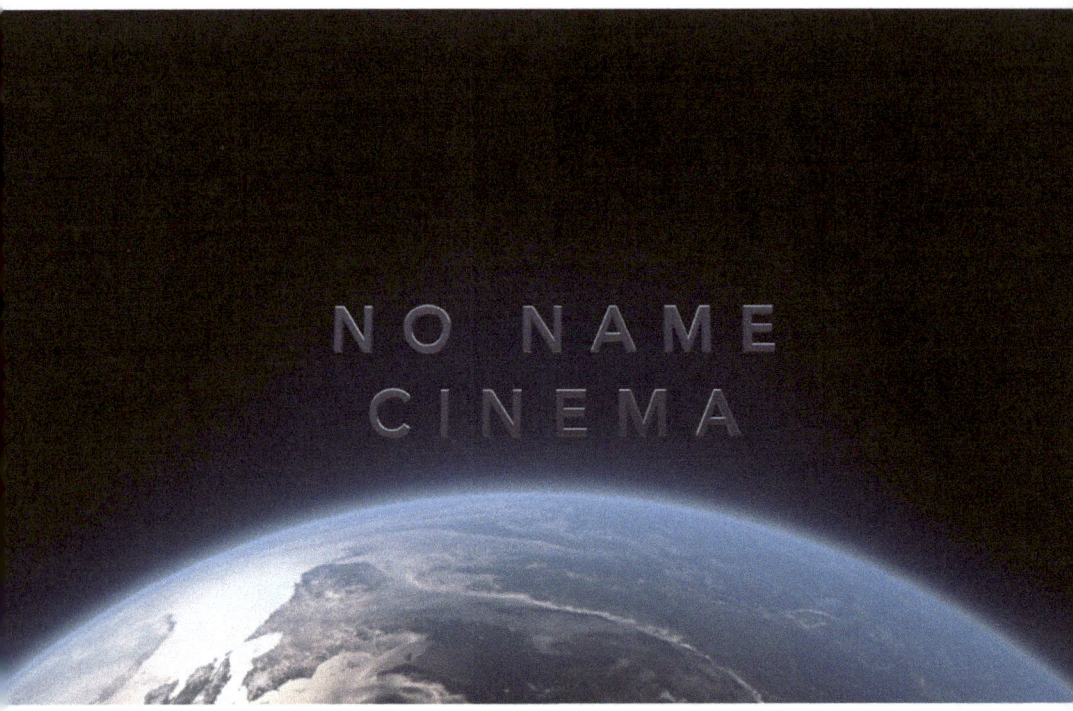

NO NAME CINEMA

MICROCINEMA
SANTA FE, NEW MEXICO

Interview with Founder Justin Rhody

Tell us how No Name started. When did you first decide to create a microcinema?

In early 2020 my partner, Abigail Smith, and I began throwing around the idea with our friend Mara Padilla. Everyone was so enthusiastic that it quickly snowballed in conversation from the idea of us occasionally showing a movie in our backyard into the three of us adding up what little money we had saved and fantasizing about buying an old dilapidated theater. Financially we were a million miles from where we needed to be, and in the light of morning the idea of renting a warehouse seemed more of our style anyway… Then the pandemic hit and all of our plans were (obviously) put on hold. In the meantime, I decided to begin the project as a monthly streaming series with the hopes of taking it into the real world when it became safe and appropriate to do so. I ended up curating about 20 different live-streamed programs that way, sometimes working with incredible artists like Lynne Sachs and Zachary Epcar. Then NNC transitioned into being a roaming pop-up screening series, which apparently can add a lot of unforeseen technical difficulties and stress. It wasn't long after then that the clouds parted and our fantasy of a dingy, affordable warehouse space miraculously revealed itself to us. A filmmaker named Ben Kujawski had recently moved to town and was open to the idea of pitching in on the bills and hard work that it took to get the space cleaned up, repaired, painted and outfitted. Those first couple months when we were neck deep in construction, we still hosted a few screenings and the response was amazing. There was much more interest in experimental and obscure films than we realized and a lot of people generously donated money to help with the expensive start-up costs.

Tell us about No Name's mission.

No Name is a microcinema, gallery and community gathering space in Santa Fe, New Mexico that exists as a no-profit, non-business, anti-capitalist operation. We focus on showcasing international and local experimental, avant-garde, underground and repertory films, videos and visual art. Our programming mission is to select works that use the filmic medium as an art form rather than passive entertainment, to encourage an open dialogue within the community and to offer a platform for transgressive and marginalized voices and perspectives. Through dedication and focus we are working to assist an artistic community in New Mexico that exists outside of the museums, beyond the schlock of Hollywood and is truly a people's cinema. Admission to all events is sliding-scale donation-based, free popcorn is provided at film screenings and free herbal tea is provided at daytime concerts and the bi-monthly Chess & Jazz club meetings. No Name Cinema is a labor of love operating in a DIY spirit with intentions to foster community, conversation, and provide support to underground culture.

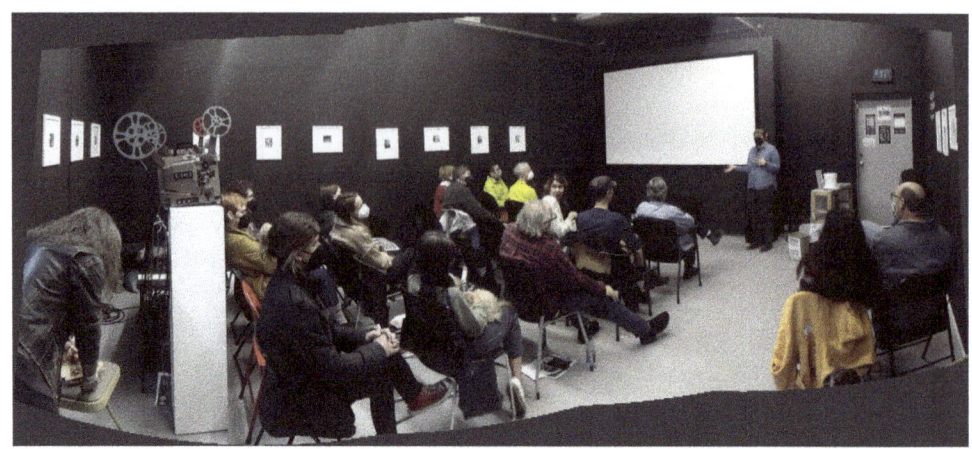

What sort of screenings can audiences expect attending No Name?

We always make an effort to have each screening be unique. We often show opening shorts that are related thematically, print programs, screen actual film prints whenever possible and host filmmakers in attendance to introduce their work or do a post-screening Q&A. Programming-wise, we mostly focus on underground, experimental and obscure films. We sometimes have to pass on great arthouse titles just because we're so limited in time & resources. We all work during the day and have a lot of other personal projects to tend to - so at the end of the week, showing a video like Jester's Rotunda by Carlos Gonzalez is a lot more thrilling as a programmer than the Janus classics we all already know and love. I want to take audiences somewhere new, somewhere that they feel lost; a place where new things can still happen.

What have been some of your favorite screenings so far?

Our first screening at the current warehouse location was of Pink Narcissus and a super-8 short by local artist JC Gonzo. It seemed like a blessing that James Bidgood [director of Pink Narcissus] felt so happy about us choosing to show his film and the standing-room-only audience turnout felt like a confirmation that maybe we weren't crazy in taking this NNC idea so far out on a limb... Since then we've been able to connect with so many filmmakers and video artists in the area that we likely wouldn't know otherwise. Our first bi-annual Open Screen event was a perfect example of that. We've been fortunate to have already hosted so many interesting artists whose work otherwise might not have had a home.

DIY projects are always a labor of love. How do you keep from burning out?

We're friends and make a point of checking in on each other, we don't obligate someone to something they don't want to do, and we regularly remind ourselves that there's no authority other than ourselves. While using

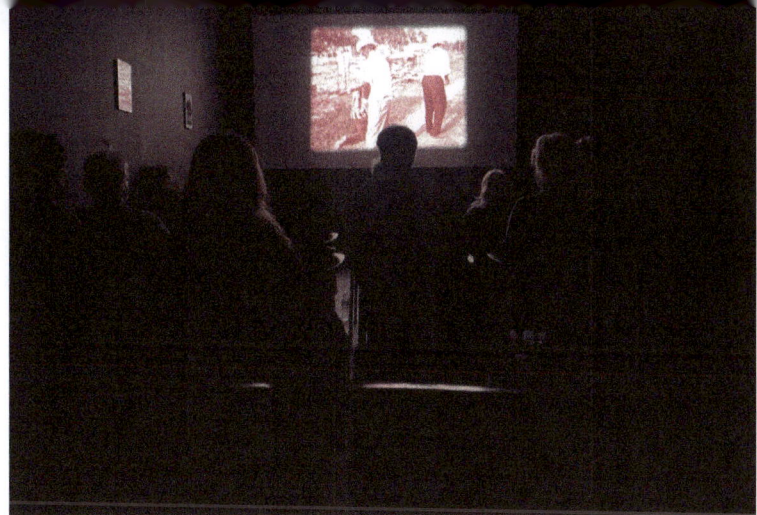

this first year to figure out what works for us personally, we decided it makes sense for us to book more shows during the colder months when we're not camping, out shooting our own work or traveling as much. A rigid schedule isn't as important as maintaining our own enthusiasm and ability to put that energy into programming.

What advice do you have for folks wanting to start their own microcinema?

Pay attention to what other people have done in the past and what's happening now. Think about what's missing. And try to find the balance between your own preferences in "curatorial vision" and what the potential needs of your community are…. Most of all just have a good time. It would have been perfectly fine if we had just ended up screening flicks in a parking lot instead of outfitting a warehouse. It worked out this way for us this time, but in the past there were plenty of shows I put on in public parks after finding an untended power outlet - and those shows were GREAT!

What's coming up this summer at No Name?

IT'S GONNA BE A SCORCHER: a Ken Jacobs retrospective, a low-budget UFO documentary marathon (presented on VHS), expanded cinema performances, director Erica Schreiner visiting from NYC to present her first feature film The Special People, Billy Woodberry's classic Bless Their Little Hearts, a full program of Transgression/No Wave shorts, and a two-day fest of Damon Packard films celebrating the 20th anniversary of his (still potent) magnum opus Reflections of Evil. We'll still be spinning records, pushing pawns and sipping tea on the first and third Thursday's of each month with the Chess & Jazz club. And we're working to organize a series of workshops in partnership with the local community college.

ANDY RAY

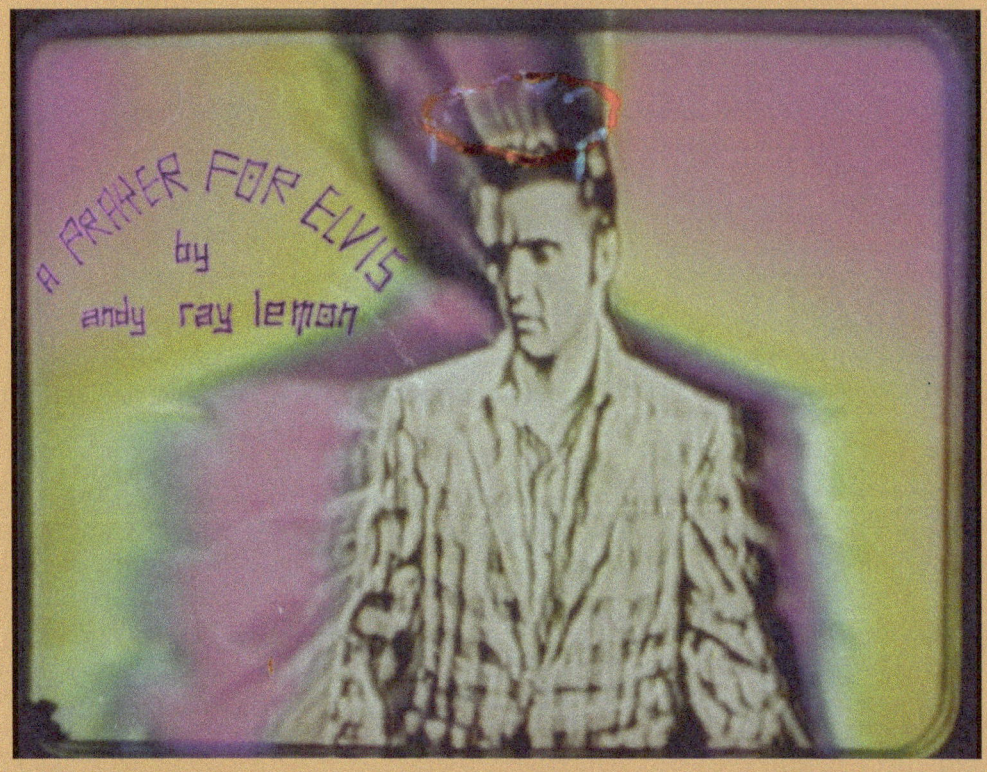

A PRAYER FOR ELVIS
by
andy ray lemon

Tell us about your background. When did you first become interested in working with VHS and celluloid film?

The first time I encountered physical 35mm prints was while interning at Troma in college when I was tasked with retrieving a hardcopy of The Toxic Avenger from the crypt-like Hell's Kitchen basement where they stored their masters in the cooler temperature, and I remember being intrigued by how the reels were almost like living bodies of media with visible histories that, just like us, will disintegrate eventually, and sooner rather than later if not taken care of! After school I worked at a video rental store in Austin that happened to be next door to a live music club, so I started shooting digital footage of the garage, punk and psych bands, but quickly got bored with the cold generic slickness of HD footage which, while it totally has its uses, seemed completely at odds with the rawness and urgency of the music. I also felt that shooting on film would help my stuff stand out more. I had a friend who would use 8- and 16mm projectors for live shows, and seeing the great textures that these shredded old rolls of random footage produced in person inspired me to make the leap of buying my first super 8 cam, an Elmo Super 110. I love the colors that celluloid produces, some of which I swear literally can't be found anywhere else. That camera was the gateway drug into getting into 16mm and old VHS cameras after that, for their vast palette of dreamy looks, and I still use that Elmo as it has on-the-fly slow motion and crystalline optics.

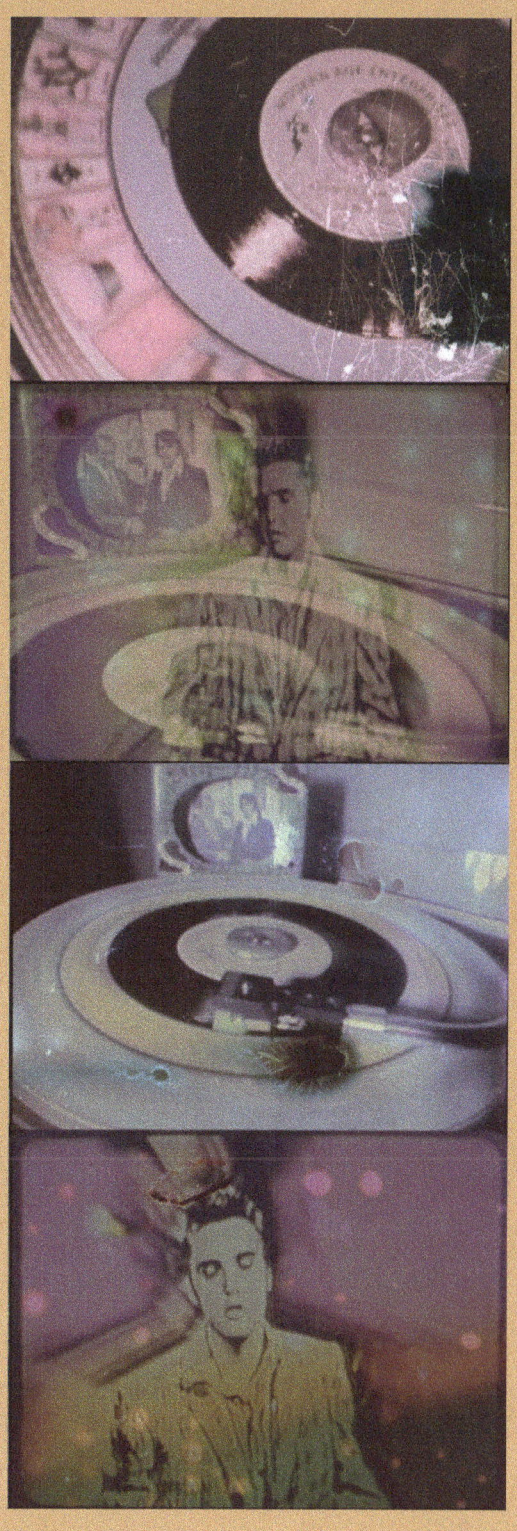

What's your process when creating music videos? Do you start out with digital footage and transfer to VHS and film or the other way around?

I typically start with analog gear, which for me usually means shooting raw footage on super 8, 16mm, hi8, VHS, or a combination. My favorite VHS cams are the older ones that used vacuum tubes, which give more of a smeary 70s public access look by bestowing an extra warm super low-contrast glaze with pleasantly lingering tracer effects. Then I take the raw footage and, if it's film, rough it up with a razorblade, bleach, heat, indelible ink, and any other violence you can commit to celluloid. For video, I'll run the tapes through any number of circuit bent glitch hardware and vintage mixers in order to achieve the right amount of distortion the project calls for, from tastefully restrained levels that just add some tactile grit and artifacts to a shot, to crude outright signal obliteration. One of the great things about workflows that incorporate analog gear is that there's no right way to do it, but each change you make in your signal flow can result in a massive difference (especially when the power of feedback is harnessed). Just as a guitarist will get a different sound when placing a delay pedal before a reverb instead of after it, experimentation with outboard gear is rewarded and happy accidents lead to breakthroughs into virgin visual territory, sometimes simply by rearranging the devices in your chain. After I've applied handmade effects to the film and video, I send the former to a lab (usually Pro8mm in Burbank) for high res scanning to digital for easy manipulation via editing software, and the latter I capture to my PC with S-video or composite converter for the same, adding minimal polishes in post such as color timing.

What's a go-to technique you incorporate into your films?

I love chroma-keying, so I often shoot with green screens or cyclorama studios for the flexibility that they provide. If one background doesn't work, just keep trying different ones until you strike on something that does! What I imagine the video will look like before production hardly ever resembles the finished cut, but I've found it's surprisingly often better.

What kind of art do you like to consume? Is it related to the medium you work in?

I'm always looking for inspiration in new (mostly older) records, books and films, and I like everything from the underground/experimental/avant-garde to pop to exploitation pulp and softcore retro sleaze. My favorite genres are anything related to rock n roll and crime. Stuff that most people wouldn't consider "art," like an 80s straight-to-video low budget erotic thriller, can inspire in its ability to convey a mood. My music videos almost never have a narrative, which just makes sense to me since the priority of most songs is mood over story. Programming the Austin Underground Film Fest for several years really helped form my low-fi aesthetic after being exposed to the exciting ways film and video could be used in the work of directors like David Markey (Desperate Teenage Lovedolls), Jon Moritsugu (My Degeneration), Bill Morrison (Decasia), Wong Kar Wai (Chungking Express), and Andre Perkowski (Nova Express).

What keeps you motivated/producing?

Music is the primary inspiration for my work, and films from the 60s-90s mostly. I also DJ and have begun making accompanying projections that complement the music. Hearing and seeing new artists who are both visually and sonically compelling motivates me to collaborate with them.

What does the future of analog technology look like to you?

It's a disorienting time because, as we move into a digital future that ostensibly connects humanity in powerful new ways, as we're constantly being told, at the same time it's also somehow alienating and insulating us from physical contact in favor of chasing some kind of instant telepathic communication ideal. But every time we make another technological leap in this direction, the tribal, archaic side of our nature reasserts itself like an ancient repressed volcano God and demands primitive, primal, authentic experience. So I only see people's appetite for analog tech and art growing all the way up to the top of the entertainment industry, in the same way that psychedelic drugs are pushing into the mainstream now because they reconnect people to ritual, one another and the Earth. Vinyl records serve a similar function and are not coincidentally undergoing a renaissance, as is VHS, and celluloid, evident in hit shows like Euphoria, which shot its entire current season on 35mm. That yearning for communal connection is evoked by and reflected in the distinctive looks of 'obsolete' technology that has been burned into the collective memory of the species over the past few decades through everything from home movies to news footage to Hollywood. The more we aim for machine-like precision, the more we seem to crave the organic, messy, and emotional reality of being human that the inherent limitations and imperfections of analog technology reproduce so beautifully.

What's next for you?

I want to further explore the interplay of analog video and film when used together like I did in A Prayer For Elvis, two forms which feel aren't often combined, perhaps for the reason that artists often just get really into one or the other. I'm also finishing up a script for my first narrative feature. My first feature, a documentary called Mondo Fuzz, was all digital. For this one, I plan to shoot lots of film and Hi8, which is technically a digital/analog hybrid, but of course recording to tape always lends it that signature saturated haze…

Anything else to add?

I'd personally love to see more analog video-related articles out there, as that subject is even less reported-on than film is within the print zine world (I literally can't think of any that cover glitch and video art/synthesis, yet new gear is being released for its huge user base all the time). In a fast-paced society of constant planning, clock-worshiping and ever-diminishing free time, getting into the Zone during the Zen-like experience of manipulating hardware-based analog video on a CRT TV in real-time can feel like a cross between surfing and meditation, and teaches you to live in the Moment. I love that you guys are keeping the analog torch burning and illuminating a field that can often be daunting to enter for the novice, but you never know what how-to technique or image could inspire a reader to take that first step of their journey into a whole other world.

www.ingramcontent.com/pod-product-compliance
Lightning Source LLC
Chambersburg PA
CBHW040111180526
45172CB00010B/1311